I0067473

CULTURAL CALAMITY

CULTURE DRIVEN RISK MANAGEMENT DISASTERS
AND HOW TO AVOID THEM

JOSEPH W. MAYO

PUBLISHING

Cultural Calamity – Culture Driven Risk Management Disasters and How to Avoid Them

© 2017 by Joseph W. Mayo

Cover Design by Brian Zuckerman
www.BrianZuckerman.com

Editing, book design and production by John Everett Button
www.JohnEverettButton.com

Assistant editing and book design by Bethany Button

Manuscript formatting and graphics by Julius Broqueza

Published by Milton Chadwick & Waters Publishing
www.MiltonChadwickandWaters.com

Printed and bound in the United States of America. All rights reserved. No part of this book may be reproduced or transmitted in any form or by any means, electronic or mechanical, including photocopying, recording, or by an information storage and retrieval system – except by a reviewer who may quote brief passages in a review to be printed in a magazine, newspaper, or on the Web – without permission in writing from the publisher.

Although the author and publisher have made every effort to ensure the accuracy and completeness of information contained in this book, we assume no responsibility for errors, inaccuracies, omissions, or any inconsistency herein. Any slights of people, places, or organizations are unintentional.

ATTENTION CORPORATIONS, UNIVERSITIES, COLLEGES, and PROFESSIONAL ORGANIZATIONS: Quantity discounts are available on bulk purchases of this book for educational purposes, gifts, or as a premium for increasing magazine subscriptions or renewals. Special books or book excerpts can also be created to fit specific needs. For information, please contact contact@ MiltonChadwickAndWaters.com.

First published by Milton Chadwick & Waters Publishing 3/1/2017

ISBN:978-0-9982410-0-5 (e)

ISBN: 978-0-9884542-9-3 (sc)

ISBN: 978-0-9884542-8-6 (hc)

Library of Congress Control Number: 2016917822

MC&W

P U B L I S H I N G

Milton Chadwick & Waters Publishing
www.MiltonChadwickandWaters.com

This book is dedicated to my wife Kathy for her gentle prodding and constant encouragement to "finish your book."

Acknowledgments

I would like to thank ISACA, ISACA Ireland and the Risk Management Organization (RIMS) for allowing me to be a presenter at their conferences. The ISACA and RIMS conference presentations allowed me to formulate and codify my position on numerous risk management topics. I also want to thank many colleagues who are too numerous to mention for letting me get on my soapbox and rant about risk management topics.

Thanks to Diane, Feargal, John, and Rob for previewing the draft manuscript and providing valuable feedback for the final product.

Thanks Bret for reviewing, helping polish the final manuscript, and overall providing excellent recommendations.

A special thank you to Jack Jones for his contributions to the risk management industry, taking time to speak with me on a variety of risk topics, providing valuable feedback on the initial draft manuscript, and writing the forward for *Cultural Calamity*.

Thank you all.

About The Author

Joseph W. Mayo is an award winning project manager, and Internationally recognized risk management expert. Mr. Mayo is a U.S. Armed Forces veteran and Information Technology professional with over 28 years of experience. He holds a bachelor's degree in Information Technology and a master's degree in Information Systems. Mr. Mayo is a PMI certified Project Management Professional (PMP), Risk Management Professional (RMP), and holds a Certified in Risk and Information Systems Control (CRISC) credential from the Information Systems Audit and Control Association (ISACA). He is an active industry volunteer who regularly participates in industry working groups and strives to enhance global risk management and project management practices. He is an author, speaker and conference presenter on topics that include risk management, project management, and quality assurance. Career highlights include the following:

- Author of *Chaos to Clarity – The Tao of Risk Management*
- Program manager for project #7 of the top 100 IT projects of 2006 by InfoWorld.
- Developed a risk management maturity roadmap for a U.S. government agency and was instrumental in the implementation of the Enterprise Risk Policy.
- Developed an IV&V program that was recognized by the Government Accounting Office (GAO) as a model for large complex government programs.
- Completed an end-to-end assessment of an enterprise application. The assessment team evaluated more than 1,900 artifacts, identified 27 project risk areas, and 13 categories of improvement opportunities with a total of 1,463 unique findings.

Table of Contents

FORWARD

One of the most important factors in successful risk management is organizational culture. Unfortunately, few organizations take the risk management aspects of their culture seriously or even know how to address them when there are concerns. There are a number of factors that drive this, including:

- Profits and operational costs are measurable in the near term, while major loss events are less frequent and more likely to be "someone else's problem" after current leadership has moved on. This is exacerbated by incentive schemes that focus on profit and cost management and ignore the level of risk decision-makers are subjecting their organizations to.

- It is relatively easy to hide or ignore the symptoms of poor risk management culture. Regrettably, it's also true that too few auditors know what to look for or are very interested in rocking the organizational leadership's boat. It takes unusual intestinal fortitude to look senior executives in the face and tell them the culture they've established (or inherited) is guiding their ship straight into an iceberg.

- Improving an organization's culture doesn't happen overnight. As a result, executive management has to be consistent and persistent in their improvement efforts, and operate with a longer time horizon in mind. This can be especially challenging in many industries because of the emphasis on the "What have you done for me lately?" attitude by stakeholders.

- Leadership is rarely provided accurate and meaningful risk information. Too often, organizations equate compliance with good risk management and/or produce inaccurate and meaningless risk "heat maps," which management has little hope of accurately interpreting. The absence of clear and meaningful risk information makes it that much easier for management to discount risk and focus on clearer goals and incentives.

- Due to a combination of poor risk measurement practices, and the points above, risk professionals are prone to inflate risk ratings just so that management will "pay attention." Unfortunately, executives are quick to detect risk-related baloney and thus discount risk reporting—all risk reporting, even reporting the problems they legitimately need to pay attention to. And, again, this is especially easy for executives to do if addressing how risk might affect profit and cost management goals, and where no risk-related incentives are in play.

Another contributing factor is that there are too few resources that focus on the value and effect of a strong risk management culture. In *Cultural Calamity*, Joseph Mayo helps to solve this by sharing long overlooked research on risk management culture and bringing to the surface the symptoms of flawed risk cultures and the profound damage that can result. He also offers sound advice on steps organizations can take to better manage this critical issue. *Cultural Calamity* is a concise, digestible, and valuable resource that risk management professionals would do well to read.

Jack Jones
Executive Vice President of Research
RiskLens, Inc.

PREFACE

Culture (noun cul•ture \ˈkəl-chər\)

Values, beliefs, norms, rationalizations, symbols, ideologies,

Calamity (noun ca•lam•i•ty \kə-ˈla-mə-tē\)

A state of deep distress or misery caused by major misfortune or loss

Cultural Calamity (adjective cul•tur•al ca•lam•i•ty \ˈkəlch-rəl kə-ˈla-mə-tē \)

Organizational beliefs and ideologies that drive bad behavior,ultimately resulting in significant loss or misfortune

Organizational culture is an amorphous element of an organization that drives people to exhibit behaviors, both good and bad, which inevitably overpowers their personal belief system. *Cultural Calamity* examines a number or risk management disasters that were driven by organizational culture. The calamity here is that risk management disasters are predictable and avoidable, yet organizations continue to ignore history's lessons and repeat the same mistakes that cause loss of life and cost billions of dollars. Examining past failures allows us to identify indicators of impending risk management failure and take steps to prevent self-inflicted risk management disasters.

2014 and 2015 were particularly bad years for Enterprise Risk Management (ERM). 2014 began with the United States Attorney General, Eric Holder, imposing a $1.2 billion criminal penalty on Toyota for "shameful" and a "blatant disregard" for the law. The Justice Department found that Toyota concealed information from consumers and government officials about defects and faulty parts that caused sudden, unintended acceleration in many vehicle models. The defective parts resulted in the deaths of at least 89 people. What I find most disturbing about this situation is that Toyota officials were able to avoid prosecution by paying the criminal penalty, but that is a discussion topic for another day.

2015 was a banner year for ERM failures with General Motors (GM) announcing that they estimate a total of $4.1 billion will be spent on repair costs, victim compensation and other expenses associated with a defective ignition switch that had caused the death of 124 people over the past decade. Later in 2015, Volkswagen (VW) admitted to installing software on several models of diesel-powered vehicles that circumvented emissions testing equipment. Outside estimates suggest this scandal may cost VW as much as $86 billion, not to mention severe damage to their reputation.

Organizational culture drives the effectiveness of ERM; ERM does not drive organizational culture. VW, as an example, has an extremely well-defined ERM function but they still fell prey to societal and organizational pressures, which set the stage for scandal. The constant clamor to increase shareholder value drives organizations to take a very shortsighted view of risk impact.

As we will see through the course of this book, employees at several organizations reported information to management about impending risk events, but management failed to take action. I submit that one reason management fails to take action is that they believe the impact won't occur before the next financial reporting cycle, so they feel compelled to kick the can down the road. This situation becomes a vicious cycle causing the loss impact to grow exponentially over time, ultimately resulting in a catastrophic loss event including loss of life and billions of dollars spent on corrective action, hence a self-imposed calamity driven by organizational culture.

Potemkin Villages also plague many organizations today. A Potemkin Village is a structure created, and activities carried out for the sake of appearances only, a façade without underlying substance (Enron, 2002). Later in the book, I will describe my personal experience with Potemkin Villages, how to spot them, and what to do about them. I will also explore epic examples including what appears to be a Potemkin Village at VW that is beginning to crumble. Potemkin Villages, organizational culture that drives inappropriate risk behavior, and corporate arrogance are the phenomena that drove me to write *Cultural Calamity*. The calamity of it all is that International Standards and industry best practices exist that can prevent high profile ERM failures, but for some reason, organizations can't or won't take the necessary steps to change their organizational culture to prevent them.

The calamity is evident, but what does this say about the organizational culture at companies like Toyota, GM, and VW? Is this culture a learned behavior, a product of the global marketplace and pressures that go along with it, or something else entirely?

Cultural Calamity is intended for people who are tired of the status quo. One of my colleague's favorite quotes is "If you don't know where you are going, any road will take you there." To know where we are going, we must retrospectively examine past problems to understand the organizational culture that drives undesirable risk behavior. Once we understand the cultural and behavioral dynamics that drive ineffective risk management, we can then plot a path to recovery and improve risk management effectiveness.

Cultural Calamity is divided into two parts. Part I sets the context for understanding the impact of organizational culture on risk management. It touches briefly on the history of risk theory and explores the past 500 years of risk management. We will examine risk management disasters from the late 1800's to present-day case studies.

Part II examines a number of case studies that illustrate organizational culture problems that have led to catastrophic risk management failures resulting in death and billions of dollars in financial impact. Part II also provides some recommendations, proven best practices, and techniques that help organizations improve their risk culture and ultimately avoid risk management disasters.

INTRODUCTION

Organizational culture is a bit of a paradox. It can be tough and enduring, yet incredibly fragile at the same time. To see how fragile organizational culture can be, let's briefly examine its rise and fall in two prestigious U.S. companies, Keane and Hewlett-Packard.

I worked in the IT industry for many years before joining Keane in 1998 as a quality assurance manager. As soon as I walked in the door, I knew right away something was different. I soon came to understand that the difference was organizational culture. Keane was my 17th employer at the time, and it was the first organization I had encountered that truly had a culture, it wasn't just something people talked about. I was amazed at how pervasive and deeply ingrained the organizational culture was.

The culture endured for decades and was unfazed by market conditions, massive growth through acquisitions and numerous technology evolutions. The heart and soul of the culture was very simple and was centered on a book written by the founder and his wife called *The Six Principles of Productivity Management* (aka *Productivity Management*). *Productivity Management* was written in response to a significant number of project failures that occurred in the 1970s. The founder commissioned a study of these project failures by an independent institution to understand what went wrong. The study identified six causes that the failed projects had in common, which gave birth to the book. There was nothing magical about the six principles; they were mostly common sense, but they described the founder's philosophy about how people should be treated and set forth a common approach for conducting business. *Productivity Management* wasn't a tome; it was less than 200 pages, but it described basic concepts that applied to any type of work. What was different is that everyone in the entire company embodied the six principles and lived by them every day. Anyone who joined Keane was given a hardbound copy of *Productivity Management* on his or her first day, and they were required to attend formal *Productivity Management* training within 90 days of joining the company.

It didn't matter if you were an administrative assistant or a vice president, you got the book, you read the book, and you took the training. As a quality assurance manager, I attended all executive management reviews in my region. At one particular review, there were some new managers and a new vice president present. After introductions, the senior vice president asked the new managers and vice president when they were scheduled for productivity management training. The new vice president said, "I have been in this business for over 30 years, and I am pretty sure there is nothing in that class that I don't already know."

The senior vice president's response was swift and decisive; he said, "If you want to work here you better complete your productivity management training before the next review." The new vice president didn't complete the training and was gone shortly thereafter.

What is important about this is that everyone across the global enterprise knew the six principles and how to apply them. Keane had operations in the U.S., Canada, UK, and India. It was possible to walk into any project in any location and be productive almost immediately because everyone followed the same core principles and used the same terminology. I managed a short three-month project where we assembled a project team of 20 people from different locations. None of these team members had every worked together before, but we instantly became a cohesive team and were able to complete the project early and under budget. This situation played out countless times across the globe and our customers frequently commented about how seamless our project teams operated regardless of whether they were local or remote resources.

Suddenly, the unthinkable happened in 2004; the culture evaporated virtually overnight. Keane acquired a company that expanded their regional footprint in several markets. There was nothing special about the acquisition, and it was something Keane had done many times before. What was shocking about this acquisition was that it utterly destroyed the organizational culture. Less than six months after the acquisition there were no *Productivity Management* books, training, or anything else one could point to and say "that is the Keane culture." Several unanswered questions remain.

Had the culture been in decline for years but nobody noticed?

Was there a conscious management decision to knowingly undermine the culture?

What was so different about the latest acquisition from the previous ones that had such a dramatic impact on the culture?

Over the years I have lamented with my old colleagues about how fascinating it would be for someone to perform a study to determine what caused the rapid disintegration of the organizational culture that had persevered for over 40 years through countless similar events, periods of significant growth, management changes, etc.

Hewlett Packard (HP) has a strangely similar story where a deeply entrenched organizational culture that existed for over 40 years was destroyed within two years. The HP culture, like Keane's, began by the founders writing down their personal philosophy about how people should be treated. This philosophy was codified in 1939 when the company was founded and referred to as "the HP way." The HP Way carried over to every aspect of the business and influenced employee behavior for decades. What is different about HP's story is that the culture change was a conscious decision by new leadership. What is also interesting about the HP story is that multiple efforts to resurrect and rebuild the original culture failed every time.

HP went public in 1957, and one of the founding members, David Packard wrote down the management beliefs he and co-founder Bill Hewlett shared. Hewlett and Packard's beliefs included a respect of and trust in employees (Elsbach, Stigliani, & Stroud, 2011, p. 5). This underlying philosophy fueled incredible innovation and employee loyalty. In January 1998 HP was listed as #10 in FORTUNE Magazine's inaugural feature entitled "100 Best Companies to Work for in America". FORTUNE Magazine lauded HP as "a trailblazer in people practices." (Levering, Moskowitz, & Solovar, 1998).

A year and a half later, in 1999, HP replaced retiring CEO Lewis Platt with Carly Fiorina (Elsbach, Stigliani, & Stroud, 2011, p. 5). The day Ms. Fiorina was appointed as HP CEO she stated in an interview that HP needed to be reinvented; this was the beginning of the end. Less than six months later in January 2000, HP had dropped from the #10 100 Best Companies to Work for in America to #43. Less than a year later HP dropped even further from #43 to #63, and by February 2002 they dropped completely off the list, never to return. There were several attempts to re-establish the HP culture after Ms. Fiorina left HP in February 2005 but so far those attempts have failed to recapture the "HP Way" of yore.

Mark Anderson said it best in 1999 when he said, "Picking her is not about technology or strategy. It's about culture." (Lohr, 1999, p. 3). Unfortunately, the decision makers failed to understand how difficult, and sometimes catastrophic, culture change can be. History is rife with examples of shattered cultures that were never able to re-establish their former luster.

The risk management capability of an organization is heavily influenced by its organizational culture. In essence, risk management maturity can be seen as a compass of sorts that indicates the level of risk management maturity and the effectiveness of the risk management organization. A risk maturity compass that points True North indicates an organizational culture that drives proper risk behavior, supports a risk management organization that makes extensive use of proven best practices, and indicates the presence of a risk-aware culture that actively promotes the identification, reporting, and management of risk.

A risk maturity compass that is properly maintained leverages proven risk management best practices and enables organizations to effectively navigate and emerge from even the most violent storms relatively unscathed and fully able to function.

Be on the lookout throughout *Cultural Calamity* for the compass rose. I use the compass rose to indicate beneficial cultural traits or best practices that allow organizations to navigate troubled waters.

A damaged risk maturity compass causes the organization to flounder in the slightest bit of turbulence and quite possibly not survive the storm at all. Ignoring or stifling risk reporting, penalizing members who report risk, or constructing Potemkin Villages are organizational culture traits that characterize a damaged risk maturity compass.

If you take away only one thing from *Cultural Calamity*, remember this.

Foster and nurture organizational culture and experience decades of success. Neglect or trivialize organizational culture and failure is certain, it is only a matter of time.

HOW TO USE THIS BOOK

Throughout this book, you'll find key points identified by the following Icons:

COMPASS ROSE

 indicates beneficial cultural traits or best practices that allow organizations to navigate troubled waters. Embrace these tenets to navigate troubled waters.

RISK HURRICANE

 highlight cultural traits or behaviors that frequently lead to organizational disasters. Beware of the hurricane because these traits or characteristics can lead to risk management disasters.

Reviewing these key points (and any other personal takeaways) and sharing them at work or on a social network is a great way to reflect, implement, and reinforce what you have read.

"

Anyone who stops learning is old,
whether at twenty or eighty.
Anyone who keeps learning stays young.
The greatest thing in life is to
keep your mind young.

"

HENRY FORD

TOUGH QUESTIONS

Would you be willing to save your car company 57 cents a unit in exchange for your child's life?

How much was your bonus the year 89 people died because you chose company profits over customer safety?

How do you answer these questions? Organizations that improperly manage organizational risk, especially safety risk and reputation risk may be faced with questions even more difficult than these. Monetization of risk impact and normalized deviance are two things that can cause Enterprise Risk Management (ERM) to break down. Monetization of risk impact tends to obscure the true risk impact and is especially problematic with safety risk. Normalized deviance emerges as people in an organization learn to tolerate minor failures and defects and treat early warning signals as false alarms rather than alerts to imminent danger (Kaplan & Mikes, 2012). Normalized deviance is a phrase coined by NASA following the Columbia shuttle disaster where the assumption was that because previous shuttle missions didn't end in disaster neither would the current one. The Columbia Shuttle launched successfully 12 times. However, each launch experienced foam loss that struck the heat shielding tiles. Overall, more than 63 shuttle flights experienced foam loss on launch but did not result in catastrophe. Therefore, engineers and launch officials grew inured to the threat of damage to the shuttle and passed off the potential disaster because of normalized deviance (National Aeronautics and Space Administration, 2003, p. 55).

Studies indicate that up to 100 near misses occur for every accident

(Bea, n.d., p. 5). Because disaster is averted does not mean threats do not exist. It is important for organizations to properly manage risk events each and every time so as to avoid normalized deviance.

Why is organizational culture so important in risk management? Organizational culture is a set of values, beliefs, norms, rationalizations, symbols, and ideologies that guide the behavior and decision making of the organization's members. An organizational culture evolved over time at NASA that led the organization to believe that foam strikes on the space shuttle were unimportant even though everyone recognized that foam strikes caused damage nearly every time they occurred. As we explore case studies throughout *Cultural Calamity,* we will see the devastating effects of an organizational culture that evolves to dismiss known risks.

The Wharton School of the University of Pennsylvania conducted a research initiative to understand how firms approach catastrophe risk management. The Wharton School evaluated the stock prices of 503 firms over an 11-year period (Kunreuther, Michel-Kerjan, & Useem, 2013, p. 36). A company's reputation or image was one of the reasons cited for stock price drops of 20% or more. Furthermore, the study indicated that it took an average of 80 weeks for stock prices to recover after a risk event that damaged the organization's reputation or image (Marsh & McLennan Companies, 2014, p. 9). In some cases, it took over a decade for a company to recover from these reputation-damaging risk events. As we will see throughout *Cultural Calamity,* organizational culture is a key driver of reputation risk events that end up costing organizations billions of dollars and, all too often, loss of life.

We cannot solve our problems with the same thinking we used when we created them.

ALBERT EINSTEIN

PART 1

CULTURE TRAITS THAT FORETELL DISASTER

CHAPTER 1

HISTORY'S LESSONS

Mountains of empirical evidence exist to support the fact that organizations and individuals who ignore history's lessons are destined to repeat them. Risk theory and the study of probability are not recent phenomena; they have been around for more than 400 years, and we will see very shortly why it is a colossal mistake to disregard these fundamental risk management concepts.

Risk theory began in the 1500's with a treatise written by Girolamo Cardan and entitled *DeLudo Aleae* (Book on Games of Chance). It was the first historical record of probability theory (Leung, n.d.). Cardan was a renowned Italian medical doctor, instructor in mathematics, and an avid gambler. His treatise presented some ideas of basic probability applied to games of chance using dice. It was written in 1550, although it was not published until 1663. Following his work, a variety of other works on probability (many focused on games of chance) were published in the 1600's, and 1700's by a series of notable authors including Johannes Kepler, Galilei Galileo, Rene Descartes, Pier de Fermat, Blaise Pascal, Christiaan Huygens, and others.

The study of probability has spanned over 400 years, and actuarial science is a disciplined approach based on mathematics and has been around for over 300 years. Actuarial science applies mathematics and statistics to assess risk in the insurance and finance industries. The roots of actuarial science can be traced back to a published work by Edmond Halley of Halley's Comet fame. Halley published a work in 1693 entitled *An Estimate of the Degrees of the Mortality of Mankind, Drawn from Curious Tables of the Births and Funerals at the City of Breslaw; With an Attempt to Ascertain the Price of Annuities upon Lives*(Halley, 1693). Halley's work included a "life table" which became the basis for computing life insurance premiums.

Individuals and organizations that choose to ignore, reject, or trivialize the past 400 years of study and research are likely destined for failure. The role of actuarial science in risk management will become clear as we explore quantitative elements of risk management later in Part II.

Warning Signs

Lowell Carr was an American sociologist, prolific author, and long-time university professor. Carr conducted some interesting sociological research in 1932. He examined hundreds of disasters that occurred from 1881 to 1928 and concluded that disasters have a sequence pattern beginning with a state of equilibrium followed by a precipitating event, one or more adjustment periods, and eventually establishing renewed equilibrium (Carr, 1932). His research was primarily focused on culture traits and the deep-rooted beliefs that develop in people, organizations, and populations that allow them to survive and re-establish themselves after a disaster. What is most interesting about Carr's research is that Barry Turner echoed very similar conclusions 44 years later in another study of disasters. Barry Turner was a pioneer in organizational studies. Turner published many works about social and technical dysfunction that leads to organizational failure. Turner's researchwas focused on three large-scale disasters in Great Britain that resulted in loss of life and significant property damage (Turner, 1976); the Aberfan disaster in Wales, the

Summerland fire on the Isle of Man, and the Hixon crossing. He concluded that disasters, much like high probability risk events, are foreseeable and potentially avoidable. He was able to identify seven cultural patterns that tend to precede disasters: *rigidities in perception, minimizing emergent danger,disregard for nonmembers, information difficulties, involvement of strangers, regulation non-compliance,* and *decoy problems* (Turner, 1976). The organizational patterns offered by Turner in 1976 still hold true today and can be mapped directly to the case studies in Chapter Four.

Seven Warning Signs

I find it very frustrating as a risk practitioner that organizations continue to ignore and trivialize lessons from the past. We have 74 years of research that essentially comes to the same conclusion: culture-driven disasters are avoidable, and there are warning signs that precede these disasters.

Rigidities in perception cause individuals within an organization to develop a *collective blindness* to problems. Individuals may recognize that a problem exists but the organizational culture overshadows their concerns. Normalized deviance is a classic example of collective blindness that, in almost all cases, leads to disaster. Compliance auditors and risk practitioners must always be on the lookout for collective blindness and normalized deviance.

Minimizing emergent danger occurs when a group or individual recognizes that a hazard or vulnerability exists but they don't fully understand the magnitude of the impact and tend to trivialize or undervalue the impact. Beware of risk impact that cannot be clearly articulated, as this can be a symptom of minimizing emergent danger.

A decoy problem can be created intentionally as a distraction or a smoke screen to steer attention away from the real problem. Decoy problems can also be created by incorrect information or poorly understood information. Ill-structured problems are excellent candidates for decoy problems as they are described in vague, subjective, or qualitative terms. Well-structured problems, on the other hand, are often numerically described which make it very easy to use mathematical models to demonstrate potential outcomes and impact based on any number of alternative scenarios, making them weak candidates for decoy problems. Expressing risk impact in quantitative terms is an excellent way to avoid decoy problems.

Disregard for non-members is characterized by behavior that is dismissive of non-members or the existence of a "not invented here" syndrome. Non-members need not be total strangers; they can simply be people from another division within the same company. A notable lack of teamwork or teams that operate in silo environments are symptoms that point to a disregard for non-members.

Information difficulties are generally associated with ill-structured problems. The general, vague, and subjective terms used to describe ill-structured problems are often accompanied by incorrect, incomplete, or ambiguous information making it very difficult to clearly document the problem, associated impact, and resolution procedures. Ambiguities and data gaps that are allowed to persist should be seen as warning signs and risk practitioners should immediately escalate these situations.

The involvement of strangers doesn't literally mean involving strangers off the street. Involvement of strangers is more commonly used to describe people or organizations that are improperly or inadequately trained. Insufficient or inadequate training can cause people to react in unexpected or unusual ways and inadvertently trigger a hazardous situation that can quickly escalate to become a full-blown disaster. The Chernobyl nuclear disaster is one of the best-known cases where improper training and inexperience were the driving forces behind the worst nuclear disaster in history.

One would think that **regulatory non-compliance** is rather unusual, but that is not the case. Some organizations overlook or trivialize regulations that they perceive to be ridiculous, outdated, or not applicable. Speed limits are a very simplistic example of regulatory non-compliance. Just about everyone has seen someone exceeding the speed limit. Organizations that do not implement internal controls to monitor regulatory compliance are effectively telling employees that compliance is optional. This quickly becomes a slippery slope as the organizational culture can become increasingly tolerant of regulatory non-compliance over time, which sets the stage for disaster.

Four Significant Risk Management Problems

The seven cultural patterns (*rigidities in perception, minimizing emergent danger, disregard for nonmembers, information difficulties, involvement of strangers, regulation non-compliance,* and *decoy problems*) are subsets of four significant risk management problems; normalized deviance, risk normalization, rejection, and deception.

Normalized Deviance

Rigidities in perception (collective blindness) and minimizing emergent danger are cultural patterns that are symptoms of normalized deviance, which we touched on previously. When allowed to proceed unchecked, normalized deviance leads to catastrophic failure. The question of failure is not if, but when and how bad the failure will be. A key point to keep in mind is that the longer normalized deviance is allowed to persist the greater the impact will be. We will see several examples of normalized deviance in Chapter Four.

Risk Normalization

Monetization and information difficulties are cultural patterns that are symptoms of risk normalization. Risk normalization is the process of modifying risk impact information to produce uniform data. It is frequently used to simplify risk reporting. Monetizing risk impact is the most common form of risk normalization and it occurs when all risk impact is expressed in monetary terms. Risk normalization sounds good in theory, but it tends to obscure the actual impact of the risk event, especially with safety and reputation risk events. When risk impact is understated or obscured, organizations tend to underestimate the resources required to treat the risk, resulting in many, very expensive loss events.

I attended an International risk management conference in 2015 and was quite shocked by one of the sessions I attended. One of the presenters said, "ERM's job is to protect the balance sheet." ERM is a function that must address *all* types of risk, not just financial risk. Monetizing risk impact and normalizing risk impact are two of the biggest problems risk practitioners face. Monetizing and normalizing risk makes it very easy to report risk exposure and risk treatment cost but obscures the true risk impact. When risk impact is obscured or undervalued, it causes decision makers to make very poor decisions. This is particularly the case for safety risk where poorly managed risk events can lead to loss of life.

If you are to ask someone "What is the value of human life?" many people's responses will be "Human life is priceless." Unfortunately, the desire to monetize risk impact has given rise to a need to quantify the value of human life. Unbelievably, in 2008 the International Standard for the value of human life was $50,000. The Stanford Graduate School of Business conducted research in 2008 that contends the actual value of human life is $129,000 (Kingsbury, 2008). Anyone who has lost a loved one would likely argue that these values are woefully inadequate.

Monetizing risk impact causes these values to be used by decision makers to make decisions about what safety controls are worthwhile and cost effective. Consider a safety risk event that has a risk impact of $2.5 million, and the risk treatment cost is $4.4 million. Many decision makers would simply accept this risk because the treatment cost is nearly twice the potential impact and it doesn't make economic sense to spend $4.4 million to save $2.5 million. There would likely be a very different outcome if the same safety risk event were presented to decision makers as a safety risk event that could cause 50 people to lose their lives and the risk treatment cost is $4.4 million. I would like to think that decision makers would choose to spend the $4.4 million to save 50 lives. Please note, 50 lives multiplied by the International Standards value of human life of $50,000 is $2.5 million. As you can see, monetizing risk impact can dramatically change the equation.

Monetizing safety and reputation risk is especially problematic because the actual impact is profoundly influenced by the emotions of juries and victims. GM established a $595 million compensation fund for victims of an ignition-switch defect that resulted in the death of 124 people and injury to 275 others. This translates to an average of $1.5 million in compensation for each victim (Spector, 2015). Toyota chose not to establish a victim compensation fund for injuries and fatalities resulting from unintended acceleration of several Toyota models. Instead, they opted to negotiate individual settlements with each victim. By October 2014 Toyota had settled 145 of 246 pending injury settlements associated with the unattended acceleration.

Toyota is understandably tight-lipped about these settlements, but some information on settlement amounts are trickling out. The victims of one fatal accident in 2006 were awarded a total of $11 million with individual settlement amounts ranging from $750,000 to $4 million (Forliti, 2015). Two victims in another fatal accident were each awarded $1.5 million in compensatory damages related to the unintended acceleration of their 2005 Camry (Trop, 2013). Regardless of whether you subscribe to the International Standard of $50,000 or The Stanford Graduate School of Business amount of $129,000 to value human life, the actual impact from a loss event involving loss of life is 6 to 80 times higher than those benchmark values.

I conducted a risk assessment for a large government agency and found they normalized risks using a concept called a Risk Adjusted Cost (RAC). The RAC process combined probability of occurrence and impact, applied weighting factors, and produced an RAC Score. Using the RAC calculation, I found that some risk events with a "High" probability of occurrence had the same priority as others with a "Very High" probability of impact. Because the risk events were normalized using the RAC score the actual impact was replaced with a weighted score and stakeholders were unaware of either actual impact or probability of occurrence. In a situation where "Very High" equates to loss of life and "High" equates to minor injury, the risk normalization process would rank these risk events equally when loss of life should clearly be prioritized much higher than a minor injury. As you can see, normalizing risk impact can set the stage for catastrophic results. We will examine a number of case studies later that clearly illustrate the detrimental effect of risk normalization.

Information difficulties are caused by people attempting to communicate information about ill-structured, complex or poorly understood problems. Ill-structure or poorly understood problems are generally caused by unresolved ambiguities. Ignoring ambiguities or using normalization to obfuscate ill-structure problems can lead to disastrous results.

The Summerland fire on the Isle of Man in 1973 clearly illustrates the danger of information difficulties. Summerland was a leisure center designed by a small architectural design firm and constructed using two novel building materials: Colour Galbestos and polymethylmethacrylate sheeting also known as Oroglas. The fire started on August 2, 1973, and more than 50 people perished. In this case, the architectural firm didn't fully understand the complexity of a design problem of this size nor did they fully understand the complexities introduced by using novel building materials. These two problems combined with a complex organizational structure caused many unresolved ambiguities to develop and persist (Turner, 1976).

Rejection

Disregard for nonmembers, involvement of strangers, and regulatory non-compliance are symptoms of rejection. Rejection is a cultural pattern or trait that borders on arrogance. There are two aspects of rejection. On the one hand, rejection can be somewhat passive where organizational behavior trivializes risk impact, threat capabilities, and vulnerability of the organization's assets. On the other hand, rejection also includes organizational behavior that actively rejects industry best practices, proven standards, and laws that the organization perceives do apply to them. We will see several examples of rejection throughout *Cultural Calamity*.

Deception

Decoy problems and Potemkin Villages are two symptoms of deception. Decoy problems can be created intentionally to move attention away from a known problem, or they can be created unintentionally by a lack of understanding. Toyota blamed ill-fitting vehicle floor mats for their unintended acceleration problem knowing full well that the throttle assembly was defective.

Improper terminology is one example of a decoy problem caused by a lack of understanding. Improper or inconsistent use of risk terminology exacerbates many of the culture traits noted by Carr and Turner. Many people and organizations use risk management terms and terminology incorrectly or inconsistently. For example, a problem that is pervasive throughout many industries and organization is misusing the term "risk." Risk is often used to refer to "things" such as risk events, threats, types of risk, and concerns. Risk is not a physical thing that we can touch. Risk is a series of forces that under certain conditions can affect our ability to achieve one or more objectives. Using the term "risks" to describe risk events, threat events, or vulnerabilities causes confusion and should be avoided. Risk should always be a singular term much the same way that energy is used to describe various types of generated power such as solar power, wind power, hydroelectric power, etc.

Consider a discussion about alternative energy sources. If someone were to say, "List your top alternative energies in priority order." It would take the listener some time to decipher the request, and they would most likely require some degree of clarification. Unfortunately, it is commonplace for people to say, "List your top risks in priority order." The problem with this scenario is that the recipient of this request has no context so they respond based on their role in the organization, which may or may not be what the requestor wants. Alternatively, it is much clearer if the requester asks, "Can you list your top safety risk events?"

Inconsistently using terms causes confusion, which can dramatically undermine the risk management program. For example, the terms risk treatment, risk mitigation, and risk control are often used interchangeably, and in some organizations these three terms are synonymous. However, to trained risk practitioners, these terms have very different meanings.

Risk treatment is part of a multi-step process that includes executing actions to reduce the impact of risk events. Risk mitigation is one of four accepted risk management strategies: accept, avoid, transfer, and mitigate. Risk mitigation is a risk strategy where a risk treatment plan is prepared based on a mitigation strategy or series of actions that are likely to reduce risk impact to some degree. Risk control is not an accepted risk management term but is frequently used in many organizations. The term risk control is especially problematic for people new to risk management because it implies that risk can be controlled, which, while not impossible, is extremely unlikely. The best that we can usually hope for is to reduce risk impact; rarely can risk be eliminated or controlled. As you can see, using these terms incorrectly or interchangeably can quickly lead to confusion followed by lengthy discussions trying to sort things out and get consensus on what everyone is actually talking about.

Improper use of terminology is further compounded by the fact that different standards bodies use different terms to mean the same thing. For example, ISACA uses the term current risk, which is the same as PMI's term primary risk. The good news is that the international risk management community has recognized this terminology issue as a problem and there is a move afoot to begin defining a core set of risk management terms many of which are being reflected in international standards. The challenge that we all face now is to effect change within our own organizations and begin using industry accepted risk management terms defined in these international standards.

Risk, in the singular form, should be used to refer to a broad category of risk such as budget risk, safety risk, or reputation risk. Specific risk attributes or characteristics can be used in the plural form to describe groups of risk elements such as risk events, threats, vulnerabilities, assets, etc. Proper usage of risk terminology helps frame discussions and drives more meaningful risk discussions.

A Potemkin Village is another example of a decoy problem. A Potemkin Village is a term used to describe situations where structures are created and activities carried out for the sake of appearances only, without underlying substance (Ingram, Underwood, & Thompson, 2014). Legend has it that Grigory Potemkin became Governor of Southern Ukraine and Crimea after the Russian takeover in 1774. Potemkin was assigned to rebuild the areas after a series of wars between the Ottoman Empire and Russia. In 1787, the Russian Empress Catherine II and her entourage embarked on a six-month trip through the area, floating down the Dnieper River on a caravan of barges. To assure his continued favor with Catherine

II, Potemkin is reported to have built a fake portable settlement along the banks of the Dnieper River. Each night after Catherine II and her entourage passed the village, Potemkin would have the village disassembled and reassembled further down river to give the impression of a thriving, prosperous economy throughout the region. However, the reality was quite different.

Many people question the authenticity of the legend but whether it is true or not, the fact remains that organizations do construct facades with very little substance behind them. Enron is probably the king of Potemkin Villages. Enron went so far as to create a fake trading floor at their Houston Headquarters and ordered staff to pretend they were "doing deals" during the annual meeting with the intent of impressing Wall Street Analysts ("Enron "created fake trading room,"" 2002).

CHAPTER 2

RISK HURRICANE

Normalized deviance, risk normalization, rejection, and deception should not be seen as warnings as much as they should be a call to action. I refer to these four risk management problems and the associated cultural patterns as "risk hurricanes." Hurricanes occur in nature every year. They are predicable, make a mess of everything, and no good comes from a hurricane that makes landfall. Even though hurricanes occur on a regular basis, damage can largely be avoided through effective planning and preparation. The best outcome most can hope for from a hurricane is a big mess that is expensive and time-consuming to clean up; the worst outcome is a full blown catastrophe with billions in property damage, loss of life, and recovery that can take months or even years. Risk hurricanes, like hurricanes in nature, are predictable, extremely costly if ignored, and avoidable with planning and preparation. Risk hurricanes can be avoided through effective risk management built on a foundation of International Standards and a quantitative data approach.

Figure 1 depicts the risk hurricane warning signs. The warning signs include four categories of cultural traits (normalized deviance, rejection, risk normalization, and deception), Turner's seven cultural patterns or behaviors (collective blindness, decoy problems, disregard for non-members, information difficulties, involvement of strangers, regulatory non-compliance, and minimize emergent danger), and three additional culture behaviors I have identified over the past thirty years (head in the sand, monetization, and Potemkin Village). We will see these warning signs play out time and time again as we examine risk management disasters that have occurred within the past ten years. These culture traits can have endless variations. These four traits and their associated behaviors require observation and analysis to determine whether or not they are truly based on organizational culture. It is very unlikely that one can walk into an organization and immediately identify one or more of these cultural traits or patterns. Based on my experience, these cultural traits can easily be identified over a period of months; it doesn't take years of observation and analysis to identify these organizational behaviors.

Be on the lookout for the hurricane symbol throughout *Cultural Calamity*. I use the hurricane symbol to highlight cultural traits that frequently lead to a risk hurricane.

Figure 1: Risk Hurricane Warning Signs

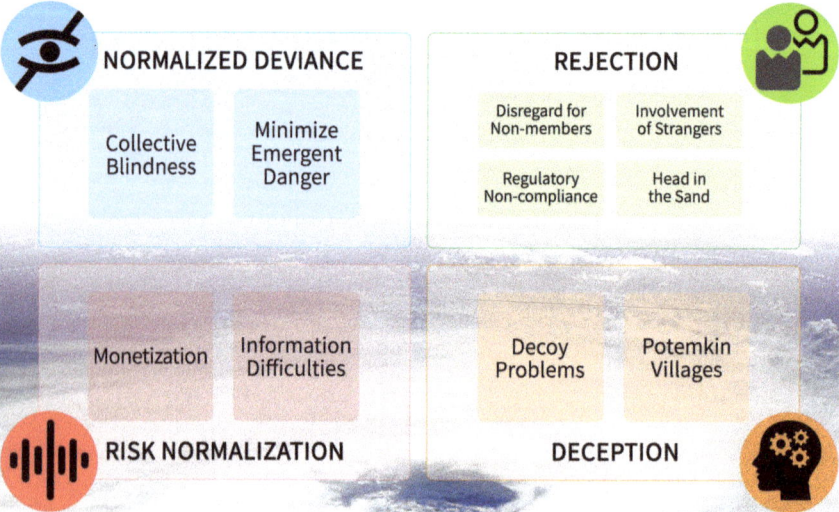

CHAPTER 3

CLASH OF CULTURES

Speaking at International Risk conferences has afforded me the opportunity to discuss risk management and risk culture with people from many different countries. One thing that struck me as odd is that people outside the United States look to the United States as the global leader in risk management. While this may be true in the financial services, nuclear, medical, and oil exploration industries, it couldn't be farther from reality in other industries. It became quite clear in my discussions with global risk managers that countries and cultures outside the Unites States have a more comprehensive and cohesive risk management approach than most U.S. based companies. I also noted that risk managers outside the U.S. have a clear understanding of risk terminology, concepts, and overall a much better understanding of risk management than their counterparts in the U.S. This phenomenon is a key driving force behind many of my conference presentations and this book.

Initially, I set out to conduct research to understand why people from other countries seem to have a more comprehensive understanding of risk management than people in the United States. I sought to understand the driving force behind this risk-aware culture outside the United States. I also wanted to learn why there was this perception that all organizations in the United States had robust and highly sophisticated risk management practices.

Through the course of my research, I found three definitive sources that answer my questions about organizational culture and how it affects an organization's ability to effectively manage risk.

The first source is the aforementioned research paper published by Barry Turner in 1976 that analyzed three low-tech disasters and identified the seven common characteristics that caused a series of disasters (Turner, 1976). The second source is a dissertation published by Carolyn Libuser in 1994 that presents an organizational model that allows organizations to avoid catastrophic failure (Libuser, 1994). Finally, the third source is a collection of documents from the European Union (EU).

Libuser pointed out that U.S. disaster literature largely ignored Turner's research. The propensity of U.S. risk managers tend to ignore risk management research which is consistent with findings by Lofstedt, Ikeda, and Thompson whose research indicates that U.S. risk decisions are primarily driven by political and legal precedents instead of scientific or empirical research (Lofstedt, Ikeda, Thompson, 2000). The Deepwater Horizon disaster in 2010 is an excellent example where political precedent trumped scientific research. British Petroleum (BP) was required to submit an Oil Spill Response Plan that included worst-case spill scenarios when they applied for their drilling permit. This plan presented worst-case spill scenarios ranging from 28,033 to 250,000 barrels (Davis, 2012). Between 1937 and 2010 there were at least 59 oil spills worldwide ranging from 29,000 barrels to 6 million barrels. The top 10 spills ranged from 1 - 6 million barrels and averaged 2.3 million barrels. BP acknowledged that deep-water drilling in the Gulf of Mexico was high risk. It is inconceivable to me that BP presented worst-case scenarios that were 2,400% less than known spills that occurred in less risky conditions, yet no one within BP or the U.S. government questioned the spill scenarios.

The third source of information is a extensive collection of EU directives and guidance documents. My research in this area focused on the consumer protection policies and directives associated with risk management. A Council Resolution first codified EU consumer protection policy in April

1975. There are over 90 directives that govern consumer protection policy in the EU. There are 27 different EU risk management directives. These risk management directives are supplemented with 16 guidance documents that provide non-binding guidance associated with risk assessments.

EU consumer protection policies ensure the safety of consumer goods, the fairness and transparency of commercial deals and transactions, as well as the protection of the economic interests of consumers. They also aim to make consumers aware of their rights and the institutions and mechanisms for the protection of these rights. The purpose of European consumer policy is to guarantee the rights of consumers. The consumer policy is intended to:

- Protect consumers from serious risk and threats that they are unable to tackle as individuals

- Empower consumers to make choices based on accurate, clear, and consistent information

- Enhance consumer welfare and effectively protect their safety as well as their economic interests.

Consumer protection is to be achieved by aligning consumer rights and policies to changes in society and the economy. The legislation adopted at the EU level aims primarily to protect the safety, health, economic and legal interests of consumers, as well as offering redress and general product safety systems. (Valant, 2015, p.3)

In June 1989 the EU published Directive 89/391/EEC - OSH "Framework Directive" to encourage improvements in the safety and health of workers at work (The Council Of The European Communities, 1989). The Framework Directive consisted of 19 Articles that defined the overall scope and responsibilities of both employers and employees. The scope of the Framework Directive applies to "all sectors of activity." The Framework Directive states that it is the employer's obligation to ensure the safety and health of workers in every aspect related to work, including work that enlists third-party services or individuals. Prevention is a common theme throughout the Framework Directive and provides nine principles of prevention including

1 | *Avoiding risks*

2 | *Evaluating risks*

3 | *Combating risks at their source*

4 | *Adapting work to the individual*

5 | *Adapting to technical progress*

6 | *Replacing the dangerous by the non-dangerous (or the less dangerous)*

7 | *Developing a coherent overall prevention policy*

8 | *Prioritizing collective protective measures (over individual protective measures)*

9 | *Giving appropriate instructions to the workers.*

In December 1996 the European Commission, Institute for Systems, Informatics, and Safety, Systems Analysis and Information Assessment Unit, Major Accident Hazards Bureau issued a Council Directive for the Control of Major-Accident Hazards. It is evident at this point that the EU has a risk-aware culture that is highly focused on not only managing risk but also actively working to prevent risk events from occurring. In 2004 the European Commission issued a report that included, among other things, the Framework Directive. The report concluded that EU legislation had contributed to instilling a culture of prevention throughout the EU.

If we compare the U.S. Occupational Safety and Health Administration (US-OSHA) with the European Agency for Safety with the Health at Work (EU-OSHA), we can see that both organizations have a similar mission statement:

US-OSHA Mission Statement: *to assure safe and healthful working conditions for working men and women by setting and enforcing standards and by providing training, outreach, education, and assistance.*

EU-OSHA Mission Statement: *We develop, gather and provide reliable and relevant information, analysis and tools to advance knowledge, raise awareness and exchange occupational safety and health (OSH) information and good practice which will serve the needs of those involved in OSH.*

While the two mission statements are similar, the culture of the two organizations is entirely different. For example, US-OSHA has 57 regulations. Only nine of those regulations (16%) pertain to specific health and safety topics or specific industries. The remaining 48 regulations pertain to administrative procedures. Administrative procedures include topics such as Protection of Individual Privacy in Records, Administration Witness and Documentation in Private Litigation, Consultation Agreements, and much more. There are 12 separate regulations pertaining to procedures for handling complaints and retaliation. The EU, on the other hand, has 89 Directives and Regulations, of which 70 pertain to specific health and safety topics or specific industries (79%). *Figure 2* shows the relationship between regulations that apply to specific health and safety situations or specific industries and administrative regulations. As one can see, ensuring the safety of the working conditions of the working people is the focus of the EU-OSHA policy. Conversely, the focus for US-OSHA is administrative, and health and safety is almost an afterthought.

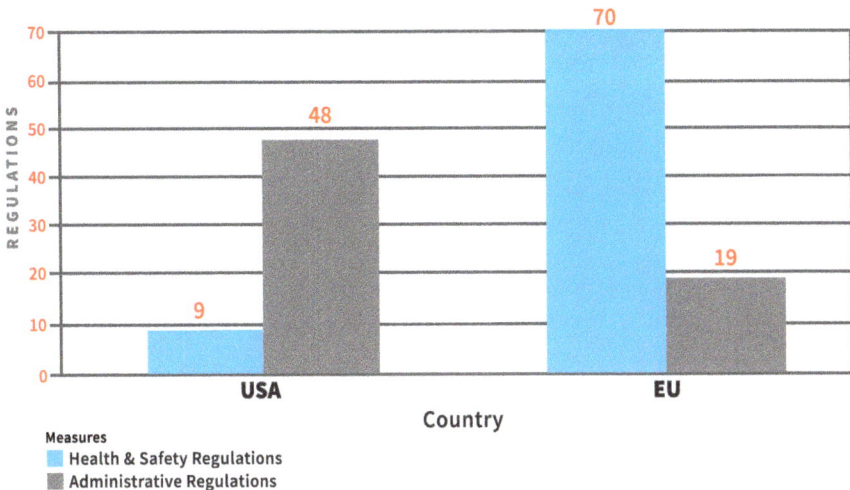

Figure 2: Health and Safety Regulations Versus Administrative Regulations

Now let's take a look at environmental protection by comparing the U.S. Environmental Protection Agency (US-EPA) and EU Environment Directorate (EU-ED).

US-EPA Mission Statement: *to protect human health and to safeguard the natural environment -- air, water, and land -- upon which life depends*

EU-ED Mission Statement: *to protect, preserve and improve the environment for present and future generations, proposing and implementing policies that ensure a high level of environmental protection and preserve the quality of life of EU citizens*

Once again we have very similar mission statements, but the US-EPA uses a legislate-n-litigate approach where political and legal considerations take precedence. The US-EPA has 33 laws and Executive Orders along with 33 volumes of environmental regulations containing 1,899 specific federal regulations. The US-EPA has one performance objective associated with environmental conditions and 41 administrative objectives. This represents a mission-to-administrative performance objective ratio of 2.4%. Conversely, the EU-ED has 18 environmental policies and 14 "Greening" policies.

A fundamental difference between the US-EPA and the EU-ED is their approach to compliance. The U.S. relies on litigation with enforcement being one of the US-EPA's top priorities. The EU-ED takes a different approach, where they have defined reports and dashboards to measure progress using five key performance indicators (KPI) associated with air quality, water quality, wildlife populations, and overall quality of life for residents of the EU. The EU-ED also has nine administrative objectives, which represents a mission-to-administrative performance objective ratio of 55%. That is nearly 23 times higher than the US-EPA. Using this information-centric approach the EU-ED has been able to reduce environmental policy violations by more than 40% over the past seven years. *Figure 3* compares the number of environmental regulations with performance indicators.

The most telling cultural difference of all is the accomplishments section of the US-EPA annual report. The report lists 41 individual accomplishments. Only one (1) of those accomplishments describes the amount of pollution reduced or eliminated, and there is no discussion about whether this is better or worse than previous years. Ten of the accomplishments represent the $14.4 billion generated from fines, penalties, and other judicial judgments. Last but not least, there are 13 accomplishments describing the number of court cases filed, defendants charged, number of people jailed, and of course, a combined 129 years of incarceration.

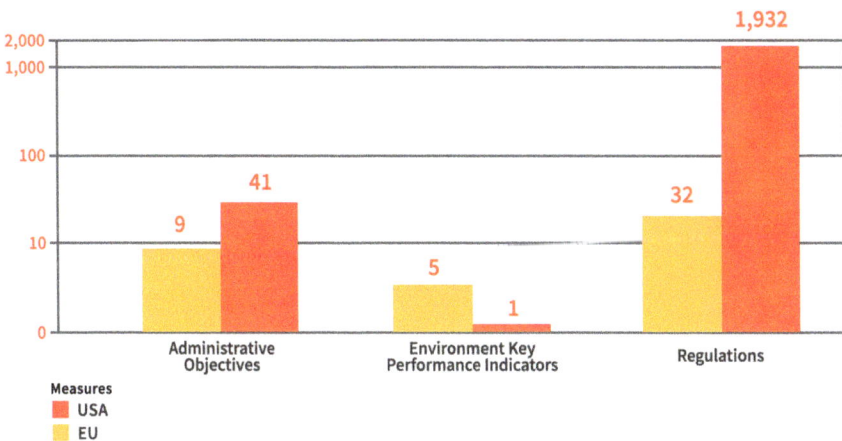

Figure 3: Environmental Regulations Versus Performance Indicators

One need only look at the annual reports of the US-EPA and the EU-ED to see the effects of a risk averse, legislate-n-litigate culture. The information-centric approach used by the EU-ED has reduced environmental policy violations by more than 40% over the past seven years. The annual report from the US-EPA, on the other hand, is a very different story. The EPA's annual report contains a chart that claims to show "progress in addressing incidences of noncompliance from natural gas extraction and production activities." *Figure 4* shows the chart from the EPA FY2015 Annual Report. This chart shows that many inspections are conducted each year along with a number of enforcement actions. What the chart doesn't show is that the number of enforcement actions per inspection is actually increasing over time and not improving as the annual report suggests. *Figure 5* shows the average number of enforcement actions per inspection. As you can plainly see, the average number of enforcement actions is *increasing* over time.

ANNUAL NUMBER OF EPA ENERGY EXTRACTION
Inspections/Evaluations and Concluded Enforcement Actions

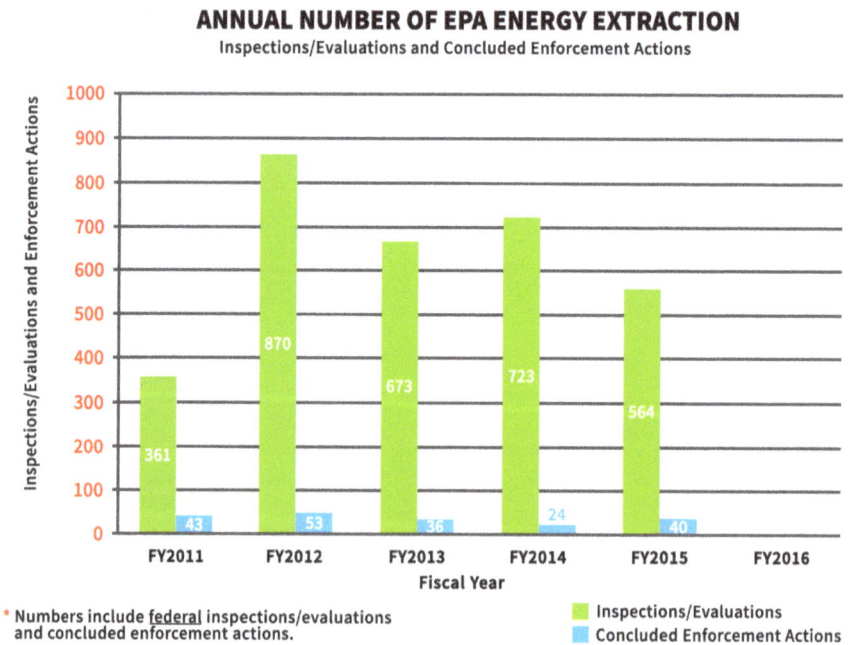

* Numbers include <u>federal</u> inspections/evaluations and concluded enforcement actions.

Inspections/Evaluations
Concluded Enforcement Actions

Figure 4: US-EPA Enforcement Initiatives

Understanding these culture differences is critical to effective risk management. Culture is a major force to reckon with in risk management. Organizational culture is a substantial influence that can cause people to make decisions that they ordinarily would not make.

We just examined two U.S. governmental agencies that allow politics and litigation to drive much of what they do. Risk management in the U.S. is also heavily influenced by these factors. Monetizing risk impact is a common problem I see in many industries and organizations in the U.S. Monetizing risk impact is largely driven by Wall Street and the insurance industry where the pressure to meet Wall Street's expectations for the next quarterly report forces organizations to have a laser-like focus on financials. As a result, dollars and cents are the only things that get the attention of the C-Suite. Consequently, risk impact is often expressed as a budget impact whether it is an actual budget risk or not.

ENFORCEMENT ACTIONS PER INSPECTION

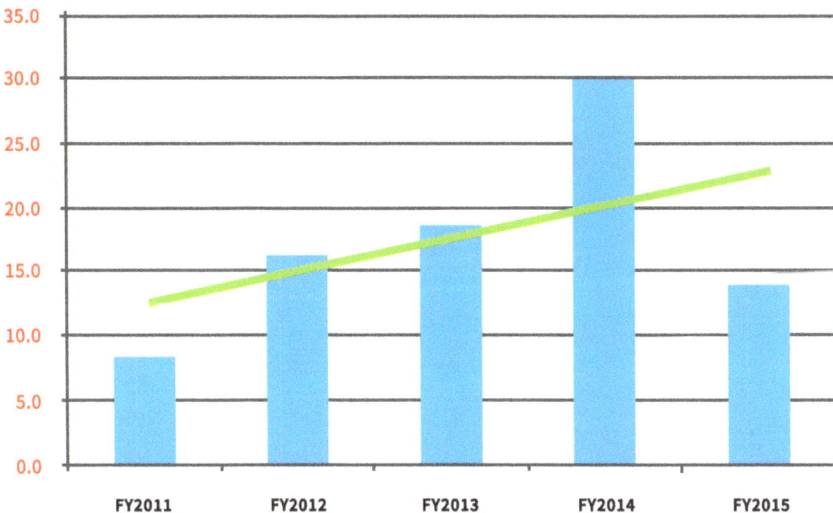

Figure 5: Enforcement Actions Per Inspection

The laser-like focus on financials and concern for liability tends to stifle innovation. *Figure 6* shows R&D (innovation) spending from the top three industry verticals in Europe, Japan, and North America (PwC, 2016). Note that Europe spent more on R&D as a percentage of revenue than North America every year in every category with the exception of

Software and Internet in 2005. Also, note that Japan has outspent both Europe and North America in Healthcare and Software and Internet since 2010. European and Japanese cultures tend to foster a high degree of collaboration between government, industry, and the public whereas North America favors a legislate-n-litigate approach, which stifles the collaboration necessary to drive innovation. Without the right culture, innovation will likely not be repeatable and sustainable.

R&D SPENDING (% REVENUE)

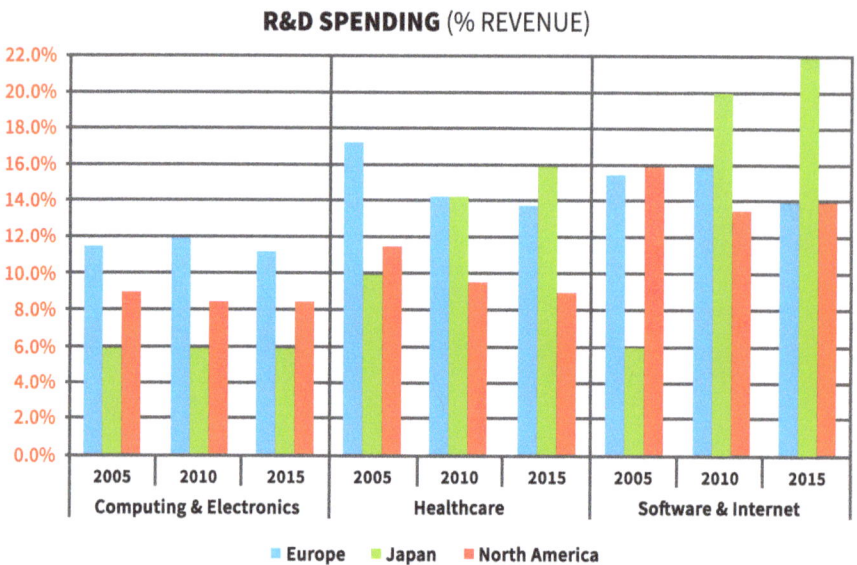

Figure 6: R&D Spending

The key takeaway here is that you cannot legislate a desirable culture. Culture evolves based on values, beliefs, symbols, and ideologies. Far reaching collaboration with an organization's stakeholders, customers, industry, and lawmakers produces a favorable environment that fosters innovation. Organizations that collaborate across their enterprise, and with industry partners, International Standards bodies, and customers are more likely to develop a highly effective risk culture.

In May 2005, British Prime Minister Tony Blair expressed concern that Britain was becoming an increasingly risk-averse society. Prime Minister Blair went on to state, "We are in danger of having a disproportionate attitude to the risks we should expect to run as a normal part of life." Prime Minister Blair was concerned that this new risk-averse attitude was putting pressure on policy-makers "to act to eliminate risk in a way that is out of all proportion to the potential damage." One of the greatest concerns associated with this culture shift is the emergence of a compensation culture, where people are encouraged to attach blame and seek compensation for harmful outcomes that should more properly be regarded as the fault of no one (House of Lords, 2006).

Unfortunately, this newfound culture shift is very similar to the legislate-n-litigate approach found in the United States. Prime Minister Blair is justified in his concern about the emerging compensation culture, where people are encouraged to attach blame and seek compensation for harmful outcomes. It is an approach that causes governments, corporations, and individuals to waste massive amounts of time, money, and energy with no real improvement in the situation. Furthermore, the legislate-n-litigate culture stifles innovation because so much of the available resources are focused on the litigation aspect that there is not much left for actual innovation.

What I find most ironic is that the Executive Office of the President, Office of Management and Budget (OMB) published OMB Circular A-123 on July 15, 2016, which requires all U.S. governmental agencies to implement ERM and integrate their risk management with internal control functions. Why it has taken until 2016 for the government to require ERM is beyond me, but that is a topic for another day. One of the most interesting aspects of Circular A-123 is that it is based on *The Orange Book Management of Risk – Principles and Concepts*. The Orange Book, as it is called, was published by the British Treasury in 2001 and updated in 2004. It will be interesting to observe the implementation and evolution of ERM within the U.S. government in the coming years. I will be curious to see what effect, if any, the new ERM requirement will have on the legislate-n-litigate culture in the U.S.

"

The only real mistake
is the one from which
we learn nothing.

"

———————————————

HENRY FORD

TWO DECADES OF RISK HURRICANES

E nron is the poster child for epic organizational culture disasters. Enron's organizational culture not only led to their demise but it also left tens of thousands of employees nearly destitute and destroyed one of the most lauded and seemingly ethical accounting firms in Arthur Anderson. Enron's collapse was fueled by hundreds of millions of dollars in off-book debts combined with deception and several billion dollars of misstated revenue. Enron went so far as to create a fake trading room as a way to impress Wall Street Analysts ("Enron created fake trading room", 2002).

Arthur Anderson LLP had been in business for nearly 90 years and had an impeccable reputation. The company was revered worldwide for its ethics and accounting capabilities. At the end of 2001, Arthur Anderson LLP had 85,000 employees in 84 countries and more than $9 billion in revenue (Smith & Quirk, 2004). In June 2002 they were convicted of obstruction of justice for their role in the Enron scandal. Eleven months later their number of employees plummeted from 85,000 to only 150 in a single location (Sachdev, 2003, p. 1). Most of these employees were focused on managing countless lawsuits from the Enron collapse and their own appeals. Arthur Anderson's obstruction of justice conviction was overturned in 2005, but it was too little too late as Arthur Anderson was fully decimated two years earlier.

Enron and Arthur Anderson LLP are clear examples of where the beliefs and values instilled by Senior Executives drove individuals to makes decisions and do things they would not normally do. Kenneth Lay and the Executive Management team constructed an elaborate Potemkin Village that lasted more than 16 years and was fueled by aggressive accounting tactics favored by the management team. It was not until an outsider named Sherron Watkins joined Enron in 1993 and saw the warning signs that the façade would soon come tumbling down that things began to change. By 1996 Watkins was working for Michael Fastow, the chief financial officer. Watkins observed Fastow applying inappropriate accounting techniques, but instead of confronting Fastow, Watkins transferred to another division within the company to escape the improprieties. Five years later, in 2001, Watkins was once again working for Fastow, and she uncovered evidence of a massive fraud (Curwen, 2003, p. 1). It was at this point that she blew the whistle and the Enron Potemkin Village came crashing down.

Key stakeholders at Enron and Arthur Anderson LLP made conscious decisions that fostered a cutthroat culture, which ultimately led to their demise. Several of the following case studies examine organizational culture that evolves with no ill intent but still results in catastrophic results. The common thread here is that none of these organizations had sufficient risk management or governance oversight.

General Motors Case Study

We will examine a GM ignition switch defect that was recognized in 2001 but not corrected until 2015. In this case, GM's organizational culture placed company profits above correcting the defect. The calamity here was that GM Management rejected corrective action proposals on multiple occasions over many years. Most troubling of all is that the part needed to correct the defect only cost 57 cents.

A GM technician determined as early as 2001 during pre-production testing that the Saturn Ion ignition switch was defective. The technician corrected the defect and continued testing. During the initial stages of Ion production in 2003, a service technician once again observed the defect. Incredibly, in

2004, GM noticed the ignition defect yet again. By 2005 the ignition switch defect was coming to the forefront within GM. Later investigations revealed that GM Engineers presented management with a proposal for corrective action in March 2005. GM Management rejected the proposal as too costly and time-consuming. Three months later, in May 2005, another GM engineer advised the company to take corrective action but once again management rejected the engineer's recommendations.

The first death attributed to the ignition switch defect occurred in June 2005. A decade later the failed ignition switch had caused 124 deaths and injuries to more than 275 others. This 57 cent defect ended up costing GM $4.1 billion in fines, legal fees, settlements, and corrective action to recall and repair 2.6 million vehicles. The recall cost per vehicle was estimated in 2015 to be $1,077. Originally, the ignition switch was confined to the Saturn Ion, but the defective switch was added to the Chevy Cobalt in 2005. Had GM taken action in 2001, when the defect was first reported during pre-production testing, the cost would have been confined to a series of document and engineering drawing updates, eliminating any need for a product recall. *Figure 7* illustrates the exponential growth of risk impact over the life of the risk event.

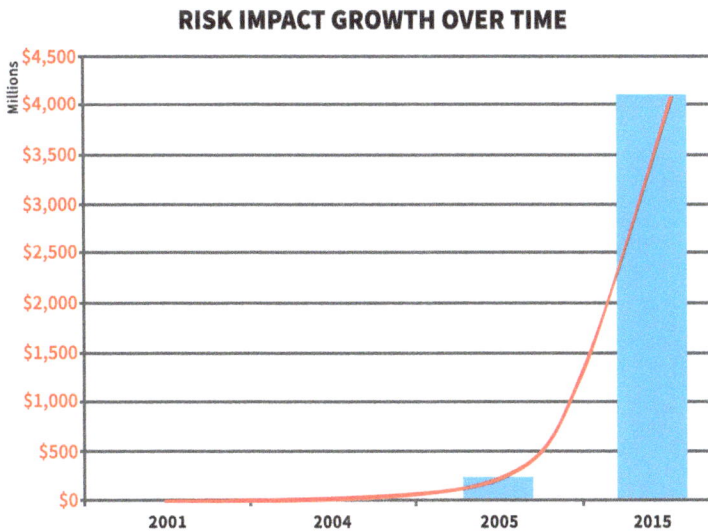

Figure 7: Risk Impact Over Time

Even if GM had waited until the second reported instance of the defect, the recall would have been confined to as few as 4,100 vehicles with an estimated recall cost of $4.4 million. Had GM taken action in 2005 with the first reported death associated with the ignition switch, they could have confined the recall to approximately 216,800 vehicles. Recalling 216,800 vehicles would have cost an estimated $233 million, which is still a far cry from the $4.1 billion it cost GM by 2015.

The timing, detection time and duration of a risk event can dramatically affect the outcome of the risk event. In this case, the risk event clearly resulted in a loss event. Had the detection of the risk event occurred prior to 2004, the loss event could have been avoided entirely. As you can see, the duration of this threat event caused the impact of the loss event to grow exponentially over time.

This case illustrates five ERM problems that are all too common in many organizations today. First, organizational culture emphasizes financial or organizational objectives and seeks to downplay risk impact. Second, organizations improperly value risk impact. Third, monetizing safety and reputation risk obscures the true risk impact. Fourth, improper risk ownership stifles risk reporting to key decision makers. Finally, ERM organizations have neither a direct nor independent escalation path for critical ERM problems. A flat risk management organization would have provided the mechanism to get critical safety and reputation risk information to the appropriate decision makers so this situation could have been avoided.

CULTURE TRAIT	BEHAVIOR
NORMALIZED DEVIANCE	Collective blindness to the safety impact
RISK NORMALIZATION	Monetized safety risk impact
REJECTION	Disregarded Engineer's warnings

Figure 8: Avoidable Behavior

GM exhibited three elements of a risk hurricane; normalized deviance, risk normalization, and rejection.

Toyota Accelerator Defect

Now let's take a look at a series of Toyota defects that were introduced in 2001 but not corrected until 2010. Toyota's organizational culture not only placed company profits above correcting the defects but they also actively deceived consumers and regulators in an attempt to avoid instituting a costly product recall. These defects ultimately cost Toyota an estimated $9.56 billion as shown in *Figure 9* and resulted in the deaths of 89 people. The calamity here is twofold. Number one, Toyota recognized and acknowledged the defect internally. Number two, Toyota concealed information from consumers and regulators and also obstructed investigations into cases where the defects caused consumer deaths. There are two troubling aspects of this example. First, the corrective action for these defects cost only $130. Second, U.S. Regulators allowed Toyota to pay a $1.2 billion penalty to avoid prosecution in this matter. (Vlasic & Apuzzo, 2014, p. 1).

FINANCIAL IMPACTS

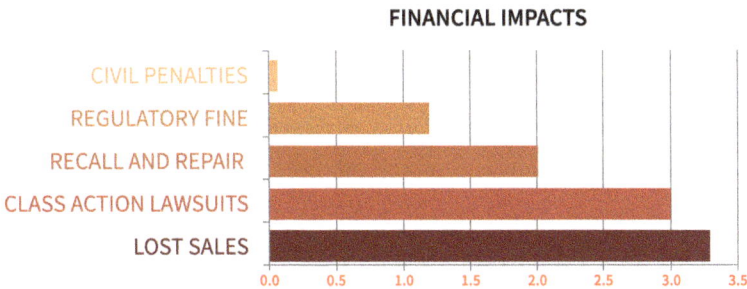

Figure 9: Toyota UA Financial Impact

Toyota received unintended acceleration complaints as early as 1992 and acknowledged the sudden acceleration problem when they recalled 10,000 Lexus vehicles in 2000 (Finch, 2010). However, Toyota continued to attribute unintended acceleration problems to floor mats for another nine years until 2009 when the National Highway Traffic Safety Administration (NHTSA) launched an investigation.

Even more troubling is that there were indications of more unintended accelerations (UA) in other Toyota vehicles. Once again Toyota failed to acknowledge these UA problems although they were cooperating with investigators. It is unknown at this point whether the UA events are lingering problems from the original UA problems that were never addressed or a new set of UA problems(Healey, 2014, p. 1).

Toyota ended up recalling 10 million cars with the accelerator defect. The estimated cost to recall and repair these vehicles is $2 billion. In addition to the $1.2 billion regulatory penalty, Toyota also paid $66 million in civil penalties. Toyota will spend an estimated $3 billion to settle 89 class-action lawsuits. Industry experts estimated that Toyota lost an estimated $3.2 billion in sales worldwide. (Hosaka, 2010, p. 1).

Toyota exhibited three elements of a risk hurricane; risk normalization, rejection, and deception.

CULTURE TRAIT	BEHAVIOR
RISK NORMALIZATION	Monetized safety risk impact
REJECTION	Disregard for non-members Regulatory non-compliance
DECEPTION	Decoy problem – blamed problem on floormats

Figure 10: Avoidable Behavior

VW "defeat device"Scandal

VW's average stock price between August 2014 and August 2015 was $198 per share. The defeat device scandal became public in September 2015. The heart of the scandal lies with VW's decision to allow engine management software to turn off emission controls when a vehicle is operating normally but turn on emission controls when the vehicles is being tested for emissions. This defeat device causes vehicles so equipped to spew as much as 40 times the pollution as without the device. Two months after the scandal broke the stock price was $109 per share, a 55% drop. When compared with market conditions and key competitors this represents a net negative stock impact of 45% within two months of when the scandal became public. When compared with competitor's stock prices five months later and normalizing stock prices based on market conditions, by the end of 2015, the VW stock price was still depressed by an average of 38%. If VW can continue to recover 5% of their stock price every three months it will still take 23 months for the stock price to recover to pre-scandal levels. I believe a 23-month recovery period is extremely optimistic because the investigation is still ongoing and the full impact won't be known for many months. It is likely that the stock price will take another big hit once investigations are complete and the full impact becomes known.

The Wharton School of the University of Pennsylvania study referenced earlier in *Tough Questions* states the average recovery time from reputation damage is 80 weeks; however, some organizations did not recover their stock

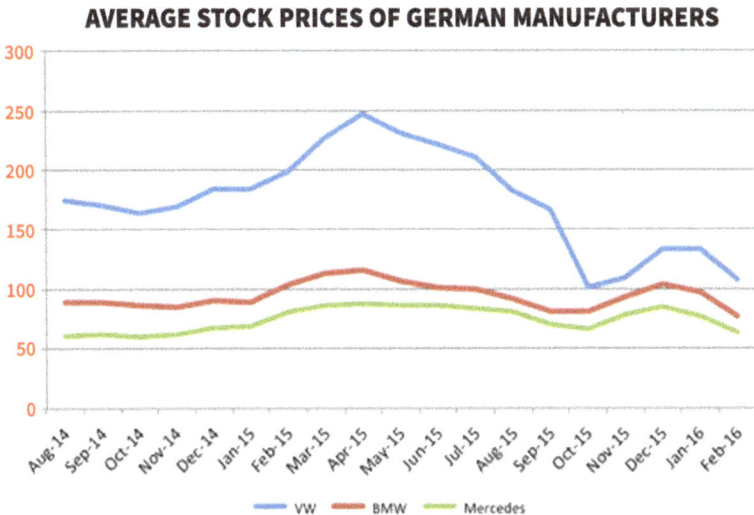

Figure 11: Automotive Stock Prices

price for more than a decade. I don't think it will take VW a decade to recover but the recovery period will likely be well more than the 80-week average.

On the surface, VW appears to have a very robust ERM program. The VW annual risk and opportunities report contains the following mission statement:

Promptly identifying the risks and opportunities arising from our operating activities and taking a forward-looking approach to managing them is crucial to our Company's long-term success. A comprehensive risk management and internal control system helps the Volkswagen Group deal with risks in a responsible manner.

VW refers to their ERM as Risk Management System and Internal Control System (RMS/ICS). VW's RMS/ICS is based on the internationally recognized COSO framework for enterprise risk management (COSO: Committee of Sponsoring Organizations of the Treadway Commission). The RMS/ICS is based on an excellent foundation and also includes a layered defense approach that includes operational risk management, governance, and internal audit. On the surface, it appears that VW has implemented a comprehensive ERM approach that goes above and beyond what is recommended by industry best practices. So how is it that an organization with such a robust ERM approach that includes layered defense, a risk early warning system, and extensive internal audit could allow something like this emission scandal to develop? We likely won't know the answer to this question for quite sometime since both internal and external investigations are still ongoing. At this point, it appears that VW may have orchestrated quite an elaborate Potemkin Village, but only time will tell whether this is the case or not.

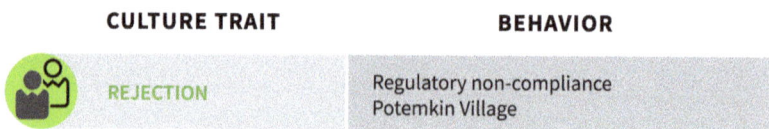

CULTURE TRAIT	BEHAVIOR
REJECTION	Regulatory non-compliance Potemkin Village

Figure 12: Avoidable Behavior

Deepwater Horizon

There are numerous case studies of the Deepwater Horizon disaster, many of them centering on the sequence of events leading up to and immediately following the well blowout that created one of the greatest oil spills in history. I find that some of the most interesting research is associated with the organizational characteristics that may likely be the root cause of the catastrophe. I see elements of these in many of the organizations I work with. The three organizational characteristics that played significant roles in the Deepwater Horizon disaster are undervaluing risk impact, lack of governance and oversight, and schedule and budget pressure.

An analysis of the Deepwater Horizon disaster indicates that British Petroleum (BP) dramatically undervalued the risk of an oil spill from the Macondo well. The Minerals Management Service (MMS), now known as Bureau of Ocean Energy Management, Regulation and Enforcement (BOEMRE), was responsible for approving BP's Oil Spill Response Plan. MMS required oil companies to present worst-case spill scenarios and describe their response plan for those scenarios. BP's Oil Spill Response Plan presented worst-case spill scenarios ranging from 28,033 to 250,000 barrels (Davis, 2012). However, between 1937 and 2009 at least 59 oil spills were ranging from 29,000 barrels to 6 million barrels. The average size of these 59 spills was 741,000 barrels. The ten largest of these spills ranged from 1 - 6 million barrels and averaged 2.3 million barrels. How BP determined that a worst case spill scenario would be 250,000 barrels is mind-boggling. Especially given that the Deepwater Horizon well was going to be the deepest well ever drilled at 35,050 feet and BP considered deep-water well blowouts in the Gulf of Mexico a high risk.

There is sufficient evidence and testimony to indicate there were significant problems with the goods and services used on the Macondo well project (Bea, 2012). Investigations also indicate numerous failures to properly monitor many aspects of the drilling and capping process. Once again, given BP's acknowledgment that deep-water well blowouts were considered a high risk, this behavior is shocking, to say the least. Insufficient and inadequate goods and services combined with the failure of numerous monitoring activities clearly demonstrate a continuous and ongoing lack of governance and oversight; this directly contributed to the well blowout resulting in the death of 11 workers and a 5 million barrel oil spill.

The Macondo well project took much longer and cost much more than initially estimated, resulting in schedule pressure to complete the well as soon as possible. Evidence indicates there were significant pressures to save time, decrease costs, and develop early production from this very difficult well – the "well from hell" (USCG – BOEMRE 2010, Committee on Energy & Commerce 2010). These schedule pressures combined with the lack of oversight set the wheels in motion for imminent disaster.

The Deepwater Horizon disaster was the result of the simultaneous failure of proactive, interactive, and reactive activities. Proactive activities are those that are implemented before malfunctions occur (e.g. governance, oversight, quality assurance, quality control). Interactive activities are those that are implemented after a malfunction occurs. Interactive activities include the ability to properly detect, analyze, and correct failures. Reactive control measures on the Macondo project included emergency shutdown, blowout preventer, emergency disconnects, containment, and mitigation—all of which proved ineffective. Research following the well blowout indicates that had even a single risk barrier not been breached, disaster would have been averted.

The Role of Organizational Culture

The dominating factor for the Deepwater Horizon failure is attributed to organizational culture. The lack of quality assurance (QA), quality control (QC), and change management early in the project created a cascading scenario in which multiple unabated failures led to the catastrophe. The situation was further compromised by budget and schedule pressure, causing operators and subcontractors to take numerous shortcuts and look the other way when faced with warning signs of impending problems. Thus, the organizational culture that developed resulted in an unrecoverable situation with inadequate and unproven contingency plans and containment procedures. BP estimates the total cost associated with the Deepwater Horizon oil spill is nearly $54 billion (Robertson, Schwartz, Pérez-Peña, 2015)

The Seeds of Failure

The seeds of failure for Deepwater Horizon were sown long before drilling began. In 2011, members of the Center for Catastrophic Risk Management (CCRM) formed the Deepwater Horizon Study Group (DHSG) to study the disaster to ensure future oil and gas exploration can be conducted in a reliable, responsible, and accountable manner. The DHSG prepared a series of reports detailing the sequence of events, findings, and recommendations. The *Final Report on the Investigation of the Macondo Well Blowout* states "…failures (to contain, control, mitigate, plan, and clean-up) that unfolded and ultimately drove this disaster appear to be deeply rooted in a multi-decade history of organizational malfunctions and shortsightedness." (Deepwater Horizon Study Group, 2011).

Robert Bea is a co-founder of the Center for Catastrophic Risk Management and pioneer in the emerging field of forensic engineering. According to Bea (2006), studies show there are 100+ incidents and 10 to

100 near misses for every accident. Unfortunately, many organizations have neither the risk culture nor robust enough risk governance to recognize these near misses and associate them with risk scenarios that can be managed. Many organizations rely too heavily on tactical risk management and relegate strategic risk management to a checkbox activity that can be satisfied by having an enterprise risk policy. Effective risk management must include robust strategic activities combined with well-defined tactical risk management activities.

Strategic risk management activities include risk modeling and trend analysis to establish key risk indicators (KRI) based on incidents and near misses. Incidents and near misses frequently manifest themselves as project issues and operational incidents. Organizations that do not have a risk-aware culture often overlook these issues and incidents as risk indicators, because there is no overarching analysis to correlate similar incidents across the enterprise.

CULTURE TRAIT	BEHAVIOR
NORMALIZED DEVIANCE	Collective blindness to the safety impact caused by schedule pressure Minimize emergent danger of an oil spill
REJECTION	Dramatically undervalued spill impact Head in the sand – ignored quality assurance and governance

Figure 13: Avoidable Behavior

NASA Columbia Disaster

The Space Shuttle Columbia disaster is a unique case study because an extensive investigation was conducted afterward and so much has been written about it. A telling quote from the Columbia Accident Investigation Board's final report states,

"Cultural traits and organizational practices detrimental to safety and reliability were allowed to develop, including: reliance on past success as a substitute for sound engineering practices…"

This organizational culture led NASA to coin the phrase "normalized deviance." Normalized deviance is a condition that evolves when an organization recognizes that a risk or vulnerability exists but no loss event has occurred so the impact is disregarded. Another interesting aspect of normalized deviance is that many individuals and groups often express concern but collectively the organization won't take action. We see this throughout the events leading up the to the Columbia disaster.

Foam strikes were a major management concern in many management and engineering circles at NASA. Launching the space shuttle requires more fuel than the shuttle itself can carry, so the shuttle is attached to a enormous external fuel tank that separates after launch. The external tank contains liquid propellants that must be insulated to prevent ice from forming on the outside of the tank. A thick layer of spray foam is used to insulate the external fuel tank. Large chunks of spray foam fall from the external tank during launch in what is called a "foam shedding event." Foam shedding events occurred on nearly every space shuttle mission. Foam shedding was known to cause damage to the shuttle's heat shielding at times and was a "high level" concern to NASA management and engineers. One program manager stated the external tank, "…had large divots of insulation coming off and impacting the Orbiter. We found a significant amount of damage to one Orbiter after a flight…"

Columbia was initially launched in 1981. After the inaugural flight, more than 300 heat shielding tiles had to be replaced because of damage caused by flying debris. Over time, engineers and managers began to perceive the foam strikes as a maintenance problem instead of a safety risk even though the risk was never formally reclassified.

Evolution of NASA's Normalized Deviance

Shuttle missions experienced a number of foam loss events and debris strikes that caused damage over a 22-year period. NASA continued to acknowledge the flight safety risk of the foam loss events and debris strikes over this time period but incrementally placed less and less emphasis on them. Shuttle mission STS-27R in December 1988 experienced structural damage caused by debris that had completely knocked off heat shielding tiles. Two years later NASA commissioned a study to quantify the risk of a Thermal Protection System failure. A review board later determined that NASA failed to fully exploit the results of this study to improve the shuttle's thermal protection system.

In January 1992 NASA allowed a shuttle to launch even though there were outstanding debris anomalies. The following year another shuttle launch experienced damage to a large area of heat protection tiles. The STS-87 shuttle launch in November 1997 suffered damage caused by a foam shedding event which prompted NASA to initiate a series of test flights in an attempt to resolve the impact of foam loss events. Five years later in October 2002 STS-112 experienced damage from debris that was classified as a "major debris event" and for the first time, no in-flight anomaly was recorded for this debris event.

NASA continued to acknowledge the flight safety risk associated with damage from debris and initiated corrective action attempts on multiple occasions. Until December 1991 NASA required debris anomalies to be closed prior to launch. In January 1992 NASA began allowing launches with outstanding anomalies, and this is where the risk hurricane begins. Over the next ten years, NASA tolerated increasing levels of damage caused by foam strikes. Less than three months after the 2002 "major debris event" Space Shuttle Columbia disintegrated during reentry from catastrophic structural failure caused by a foam loss event during launch. From 1992 to 2002, NASA's organizational culture evolved from requiring anomaly closure prior to launch, to tolerating increasingly greater anomalies, to ignoring anomalies altogether.

Surprisingly, this is not the first-time self-inflicted disaster struck the NASA shuttle program. Space Shuttle Challenger entered service in 1983, two years after Columbia first entered service. Challenger flew nine successful missions before breaking apart 73 seconds into the tenth mission. A failed O-ring was the cause of the Challenger disaster. *Figure 14* clearly shows that adequate data was available to indicate that lower launch temperature significantly increased the likelihood of O-ring damage. Three of 19 launches (15%) experienced damage to at least one O-ring when the launch temperature was greater than 65 degrees. Conversely, all four launches that occurred when the launch temperature was below 65 degrees experienced O-ring damage and the one launch that occurred below 55 degrees experience the highest number of damaged O-rings of any previous launch. Therefore, it should have readily apparent that launching the shuttle with launch temperature well below the safe operating parameters was extremely risky at best and

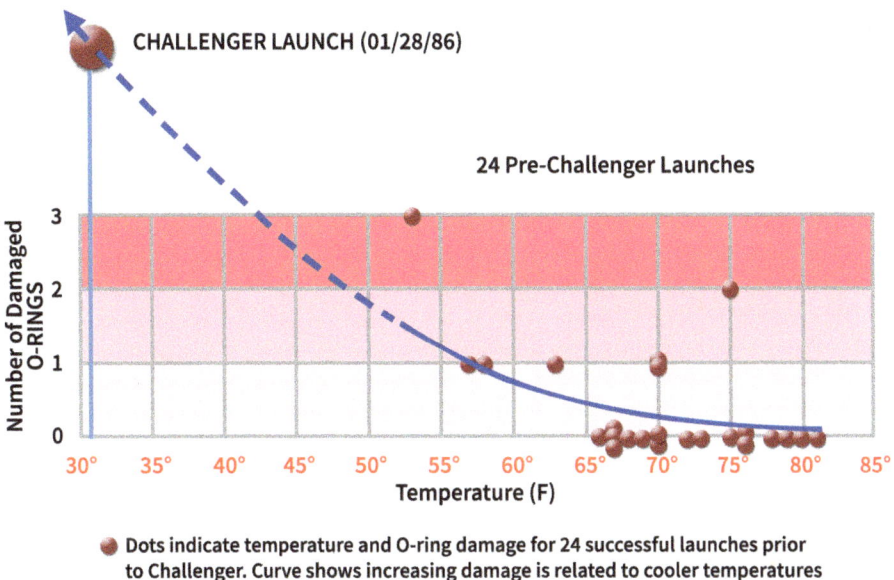

Dots indicate temperature and O-ring damage for 24 successful launches prior to Challenger. Curve shows increasing damage is related to cooler temperatures

Figure 14: Shuttle O-ring Failures

bordered on irresponsibility.

These two shuttle disasters clearly demonstrate the devastating impact normalized deviance can have on an organization. Even though individuals correctly interpret the available data and voice their concerns the organizational culture forces individuals to collectively sanction the decision to proceed. Most devastating of all is that some organizations fail to learn from disasters and repeat the same mistakes never believing the problem is organizational culture. Recall Bea's research involving recurring near-misses and beware of normalized deviance.

CULTURE TRAIT	BEHAVIOR
NORMALIZED DEVIANCE	Collective blindness to the safety impact
REJECTION	Disregarded Engineer's warnings

Figure 15: Avoidable Behavior

Government Agency

I worked in several different departments of a large government agency. Most of the people in the organization were highly qualified and motivated to do a good job. However, the organizational culture proved insurmountable. This section describes three different situations I encountered that show how devastating organizational culture can be.

I facilitated a risk assessment on a large program (> $1B) that was canceled because of delays, cost overruns, and the overall poor quality of the end product. The purpose of the risk assessment was to determine the risks associated with transitioning the legacy software from the system integrator to a third party for maintenance until the system could be replaced. I applied ISACA's Risk IT framework and risk scenarios to help concentrate the risk assessment effort.

The initial risk assessment noted 35 risk events in the risk register. During the risk analysis phase, risk events were restated using an IF-THEN construct and one of three risk contexts (Cost, Schedule, and Mission Accomplishment). Reiterating risk events using IF-THEN statements led the assessment team to conclude that 29 of the 35 risk events (83%) were issues, conditions, symptoms, concerns, or opinions, leaving only six actual risk events that were categorized into three mission risk events, two schedule risk events, and one cost risk event.

Mission risk events were quantified based on their impact on operational requirements and the concept of operations (CONOPS) document. Schedule risks were quantified using actual performance data. Cost risks were quantified using actual performance data and validated using independent industry research.

Results from static code analysis were used to validate software complexity. The static code analysis team was able to process approximately 4.8 static code flags per hour on NASA and DOD software but was only able to process 1.6 static code flags per hour with the software on this program. The difference between 4.8 and 1.6 code flags per hour represented a 67.5% productivity loss due to code complexity, lack of documentation, inaccurate documentation, and other environmental complexities.

Actual performance data and independent industry research were used to determine the impact on the single budget risk, and was stated as follows:

IF unreported software defects are not corrected, THEN maintenance costs will increase by $31M.

Actual effort data from completed enhancement requests was used to calculate the average effort per enhancement request. This actual effort was combined with unreported defects identified during static code analysis. Static code analysis indicated the code base contained approximately 2,229 unreported software defects.

*142.7 hours * 2,229 defects = 318,078.3 hours of effort to correct all of the unreported defects*

A billing rate of $95 per hour was used for cost analysis purposes. Multiplying $95 per hour times the 318,078 hours of effort results in a total risk exposure of $30.2 million associated with the unreported software defects. The customer considered this figure preposterous, so the assessment team then used independent industry data to validate the risk exposure. Industry research data from B. Boehm and V. Basili was used to confirm the budget risk. Boehm and Basili's research shows the cost of fixing a defect found in Requirements phase is $139, Design phase is $455, Coding phase is $977, Testing phase is $7,136, and Maintenance phase is $14,102 (KPMG, 2009). The software for this program had already been deployed and was in the maintenance phase. Multiplying the 2,229 defects by $14,102 equals $31,433,358, which confirms the budget risk ranges between $30 million to $31 million. Stakeholders would not acknowledge the risk stating "that amount of risk is impossible" resulting in acceptance, by default, of $30.2M in risk exposure. The unfortunate result of this default acceptance was significant money spent deploying emergency fixes as they encountered countless system failures. It is estimated that over $20M was spent to correct less than ten percent of the outstanding software defects. The calamity of this situation is that approximately 40% of the outstanding defects were a single class of defect that could have been corrected for an estimated $4M, reducing risk exposure from $30.2M to $18M, an ROI of 3:1. Had stakeholders acknowledged the risk and developed a treatment plan they could have reduced their exposure by 40% and not wasted $20M with effectively no risk reduction or system improvement.

Another department was procuring commercial off-the-shelf (COTS) systems. The code analysis team had the ability to also scan commercial software without violating any proprietary rights or reverse engineering restrictions. I presented this case to the Lead Engineer and explained that we could identify software vulnerabilities and give them other information about the overall quality of the software they were procuring. I was quite surprised that the Lead Engineer was completely uninterested. I scheduled another meeting to revisit the topic of risk reduction because I found it hard to believe that the program wasn't interested in knowing the software vulnerabilities that were present in the software before they spent tens of millions of dollars on hardware and software. During the next meeting, I asked the Lead Engineer flat out, "Why don't you want to know about software defects and vulnerabilities before you spend a small fortune?" I was even more shocked by his reply. He said, "Because if I know about problems, then I have to do something about them." I was speechless at that point and our meeting ended shortly thereafter.

I was somewhat hopeful when the organization began to have quarterly management reviews because the agenda included risk management. My initial thought was, "FINALLY, there could be light at the end of the tunnel." One of the program managers my team supported prepared his slides for the quarterly review and included about a dozen risk items for discussion. Unfortunately, the program manager was not well prepared for the management review and was unable to answer questions about the risk items on his slides. Consequently, the PMO director chastised him quite severely about his risk slides and strongly urged him to be better prepared for the next review.

The program manager's reaction was bizarre, to say the least. He announced that the program no longer had any risk events, only opportunities, and instructed all risk items to be closed in the risk register and to replace them with opportunities. Given the level of attention and questions posed by the PMO director, I suggested that this might be the wrong approach. Nevertheless, all risk items were converted to opportunities.

As the next quarterly review approached, I began to feel sorry for the program manager because I expected the PMO director to go off the deep end when she learned how the program manager handled the risk slides. I was completely stunned by what happened at the quarterly review. The program manager had a single slide simply stating there were no outstanding risk items. The PMO director complimented the program manager on eliminating risk on his program, and that was that. This behavior clearly points to a risk maturity compass that is severely misaligned and an organizational culture that prefers to ignore risk instead of identifying and managing risk.

These three events clearly show that the organization wanted nothing to do with risk reporting. Everyone in the organization was conditioned to avoid recording any risk. Even though the organization encountered massive budget overruns and schedule delays measured in years, not days or months, they were content to keep the status quo. What is most interesting about this organization is they went to great lengths to ignore anything risk related, but they also spent a fair amount of time, money and effort to construct a Potemkin Village of sorts.

The organization spent five years developing and implementing a risk policy. Following approval of the risk policy, they spent a significant amount of money to purchase an Enterprise Risk Management (ERM) software package. Everyone received risk management training and risk managers diligently entered information into the ERM tool. In addition to effectively ignoring risk management principles, they wasted a tremendous amount of time and money to construct and maintain a risk management façade that was completely ineffective.

This organizational culture is the definition of a cultural calamity. The organization had all the right tools in place: risk policy, risk management plans, risk management training, ERM tool, and quantitative risk impact. However, the organizational culture drove its members to go through the risk management motions but avoid identifying, reporting, analyzing, and treating risks. The result is that the organization had set itself up to accept every risk and waste a tremendous amount of time, money, and resources with literally no benefit.

CULTURE TRAIT	BEHAVIOR
NORMALIZED DEVIANCE	Collective blindness to the poor software quality
RISK NORMALIZATION	Qualitative risk impact measures
REJECTION	Head in the sand Potemkin Village Disregard for non-members
DECEPTION	Decoy problems – characterize all risk events as opportunities

Figure 16: Avoidable Behavior

"

In the field of observation,
chance favors
the prepared mind.

"

LOUIS PASTEUR

Lecture, University of Lille
7 December 1854

PART 2

NAVIGATING
RISK HURRICANES

CHAPTER 5

RISK MATURITY COMPASS ENABLERS

The best defense against risk hurricanes is a risk maturity compass pointing True North. For a risk maturity compass to point True North, an organization must have an organizational culture that encourages proper risk behavior and an effective risk management program. Proper risk behavior can only exist within an organizational culture that encourages risk reporting and rewards individuals for exhibiting proper risk aware behavior. This chapter describes risk maturity enablers that can help organizations mature their risk culture and establish a thriving risk management environment.

Organizational Structure

In the late 1990s, I accepted a position as a quality assurance (QA) manager for a global professional services firm. The QA organization was created to manage budget and reputation risk after a series of expensive project failures. It had only recently been formed when I joined so I had the opportunity to see both the organization and the organizational culture evolve over a period of about ten years or so.

The company had a traditional organizational structure with a typical

C-suite, senior vice presidents, regional vice presidents, vice presidents, managing directors, directors, and delivery managers. The QA organization was a very flat organization comprised of a QA director and QA managers. The QA director reported directly to the CEO. This structure upset many people in the organization because you effectively had a QA director who was a peer to a senior vice president

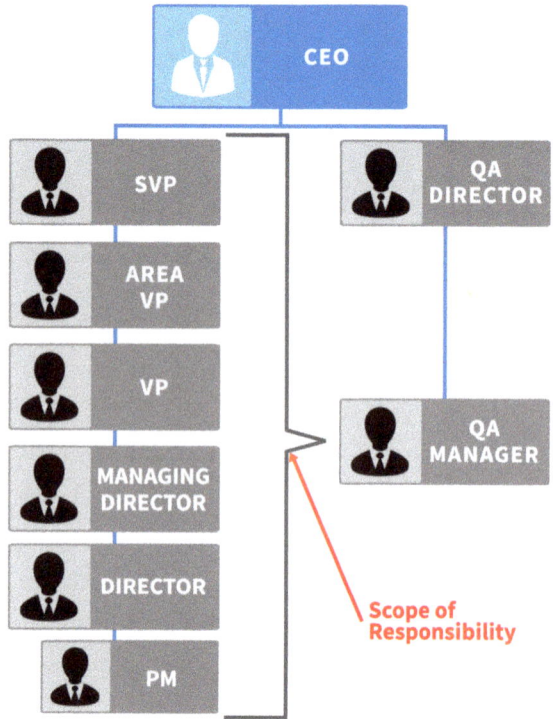

Figure 17: QA Organization

and QA managers who were higher in the organization than two levels of vice presidents. Consequently, there was little buy-in and cooperation from the organization in the beginning. However, within a couple of years, the buy-in and cooperation changed dramatically.

The QA director implemented a standard where a QA manager audited every project in the entire company every quarter. The audits examined process compliance, but the focus was to identify and mitigate budget and reputation risk. In addition to reviewing documentation and project artifacts, the QA managers also conducted face-to-face interviews with all project stakeholders including the customer. The lack of buy-in caused several regions and directors to set up Potemkin Villages where they created a fragile façade of the requisite process documents and prepared interview scripts for everyone, so there was no discrepancy between the artifacts and individual interviews. A cursory examination of the process documentation, project artifacts, and a few interviews would give the impression that everything was in order. However, minimal probing and a few well-crafted open-ended questions caused these Potemkin Villages to quickly come tumbling down. When creation dates for an entire quarter worth of project artifacts are within a few days of the audit, it is clear there is an attempt to orchestrate the audit results instead of allowing performance to speak for itself.

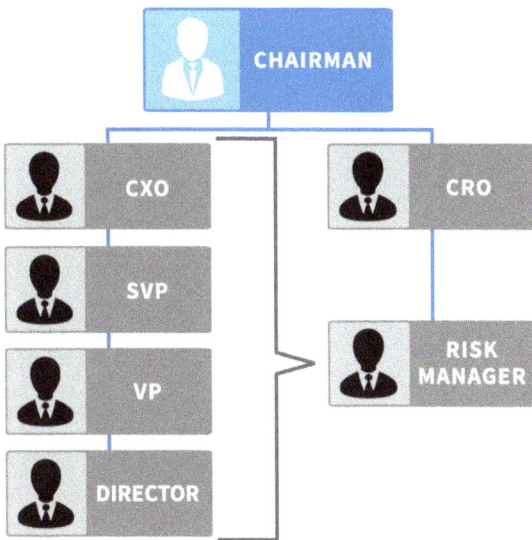

Figure 18: ERM Structure

The QA organization battled these challenges for a few years, but people quickly began to realize that the attention of the QA organization was focused on managing risk more than anything else. Vice presidents and directors soon realized that the flat structure of the QA organization gave them an avenue to escalate risk events that historically were suppressed by some senior and regional vice presidents. Once people came to the realization that they had a direct path to the top of the organization that included anonymity, QA managers became very popular.

Based on the lessons learned as a QA manager I firmly believe that a flat risk management organization structure similar to what was described above can benefit many organizations. *Figure 18* shows a flat risk management organizational structure that can help overcome the effects of rejection or deception. We can clearly see how a flat risk organization such as this would have helped GM and Toyota avoid the loss of life and billions in financial impact from the defective ignition switch and unintended acceleration problems. A flat organizational structure combined with a good risk policy, transparency, and a governance structure that drives effective decision-making demonstrates that an organization values effective risk management over fiefdoms and indicates a high level of risk management maturity.

Embrace Collective Learning

Collective learning occurs when competitors, suppliers, regulators and customers collaborate for the benefit of all. The air travel industry is an excellent example where airlines, airplane manufacturers, air transport authorities, industry experts, inspectors, and anyone involved in the industry all collaborate to make air travel safer. Accidents, near-misses, equipment failures, and procedural problems that are seen as a threat to safe air travel are thoroughly investigated. The results of these investigations are shared with suppliers, manufacturers, regulators, and operators so everyone can benefit. This contingency reserve has made air travel the safest mode of transportation in the world. Collective learning was also rapidly embraced with the emergence of cyber security. Software developers, governments, individuals, and even hackers themselves help identify and manage new cyber security threats.

Granted, the stakes are clearly much higher in the air travel industry than say the retail industry. However, other industries can benefit from collective learning even if it is based on publicly available information.

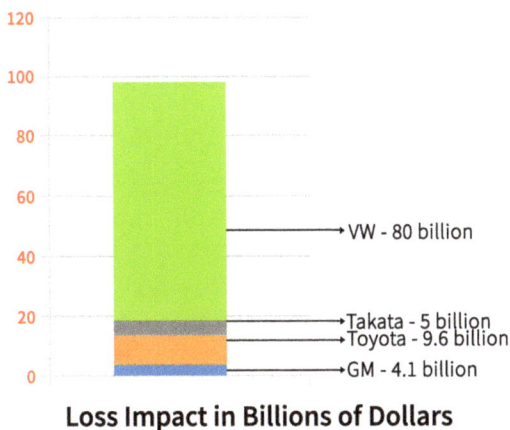

Loss Impact in Billions of Dollars

Figure 19: Auto Industry Loss Impact

Industries that do not practice collective learning on some level are destined to repeat the same mistakes over and over again. The auto manufacturing industry is one example where collective learning is not practiced and has resulted in over $100 billion is loss events during 2014 – 2015. General Motors was aware of an ignition switch defect but continued to produce defective automobiles from 2004 – 2014. Toyota was aware of a defective part that caused sudden unintended acceleration. Takata is an automotive airbag manufacturer that produced more than 100 million defective airbags (Consumer Reports, 2016). Volkswagen installed software that fooled emission-testing devices to think that harmful emissions were 40 times less than they were. *Figure 19* illustrates that the combined loss impacts of these four industry events total nearly $100 billion. . Unfortunately, these defective parts also led to several hundred deaths and serious injuries to hundreds more. The lesson to be learned here is that if safety risk is allowed to persist for an extended period of time, the impact can be catastrophic. Had these companies participated in collective learning they could have avoided tens of billions of losses, saved lives, and dramatically improved automobile safety.

So the real question is, "Why can't collective learning be practiced in other industries such as retail, manufacturing, etc.?" Collective learning clearly can be achieved even in highly competitive industries such as the aeronautical industry. Although it is much easier to benefit from collective learning with industry-wide collaboration, collective learning can be achieved even without industry collaboration. We live in a globally data rich environment where data is available from countless sources. Leveraging "big data" allows organizations to achieve a certain amount of collective learning. Risk practitioners must drive collective learning in all organizations and strive to integrate collective learning with the organizational risk policy. Collective learning indicates a high level of risk management maturity and is one of the most valuable techniques for risk practitioners. Collective learning can help avoid normalized deviance, rejection, and deception.

Effectiveness Versus Efficiency

Over the past several decades I have seen many organizations that have extremely **efficient** risk management processes that do not translate to **effective** risk management. Efficiency is defined as the ability to accomplish a job with a minimum expenditure of time and effort. Effectiveness is defined as success in producing a desired result. Risk management effectiveness is more important than risk management efficiency. That is not to say that efficiency is utterly forsaken. Effective risk management includes proper risk prioritization, balancing resources needed to treat risk with the value of the asset or business objective, and setting appropriate risk management objectives. Effectiveness is valued over efficiency because the most critical risks often have catastrophic effects if they occur, so the time and effort spent managing the risk often pales in comparison to the impact of the risk. However, risk practitioners should not perceive this as carte blanche to foolishly expend endless resources. Risk treatment must constantly be balanced with organizational goals and objectives as well as available resources.

Standards bodies strive to drive efficiency into processes and expect efficiency to translate into effectiveness. Process efficiency can translate to effectiveness in cases where there is a finite set of variables and outcomes such as a manufacturing process. Risk events have a nearly infinite set of variables making it very difficult to optimize the risk management process. Furthermore, a single risk can have catastrophic effects, so a balanced, highly effective risk management process that reliably treats risk events is far more valuable than a highly optimized process that may be untested or less reliable; hence, the focus on effectiveness over efficiency.

Risk Exposure Beyond Loss Events

Recognize that safety and reputation risk have a lifecycle that goes well beyond the loss event. The earlier case studies clearly showed the residual effect and exponential increase in risk exposure when safety and reputation risk events were not effectively managed. The GM case, in particular, demonstrated that safety risk was identified, and risk mitigation was identified numerous times but never implemented. Had GM implemented the risk mitigation they could have limited their total exposure to a few thousand dollars and fully mitigated the risk impact prior to the product release. The calamity here is that GM knowingly produced defective products for more than a decade that resulted in the death of more than 124 people, injured scores more, and realized a financial impact exceeding $4 billion.

High-Reliability Organization (HRO)

The HRO paradigm was developed by a group of researchers at the University of California, Berkeley, to capture common operational aspects among organizations that operate in high-risk environments such as aircraft carriers, commercial aviation, and nuclear power (Sutcliffe, 2011). Sutcliffe suggests that HROs organize in ways that increase the quality of attention across the organization, thereby enhancing people's alertness and awareness to details. Sutcliffe goes on to state that alertness and awareness allow people and organizations to detect subtle ways in which contexts vary and to call for contingent responses. This alertness-and-awareness culture forms a basis for individuals to interact continuously as they develop, refine and update a shared understanding of the situation they face and for their ability to act on that understanding.

According to Bea (2011), Carolyn Libuser analyzed five prominent failures: the Chernobyl nuclear plant, Exxon Valdez grounding, Bhopal gas leak, Challenger explosion, and the Hubble Telescope mirror grinding error. The results of Libuser's research indicate HROs exhibit five organizational characteristics that other organizations do not. HROs have extensive process auditing procedures, reward systems that encourage risk-mitigating behavior, quality standards that exceed industry standards, the ability to assess risk events correctly, and a strong command and control organization. Successful HROs are preoccupied by failure, are reluctant to simplify interpretations, are sensitive to operational situations, are committed to resilience and under-specification of structure (Bea, 2012).

CHAPTER 6

ASSET-ORIENTED RISK MANAGEMENT

A New Paradigm

Effective risk management is all about minimizing the impact of risk against organizational objectives and assets. Assets are what organizations use to meet their goals and objectives. An asset is anything that may be affected whereby its value is diminished (The Open Group, 2014, p. 29). Assets include personnel, customers, intellectual property, facilities, and much more. Threats are anything capable of harming an asset and/or an organization (The Open Group, 2014, p. 14). The quantitative nature of asset-oriented risk management makes it an excellent way to avoid normalized deviance, risk normalization, and deception.

An effective risk management program is built on a solid foundation consisting of a risk policy, governance, and control environment. The risk policy establishes the operating parameters of risk management including risk management objectives, risk appetite, risk tolerance, resources needed to manage risk, and overall framework for managing risk. Governance establishes a structure for making well-informed, risk-based decisions. The governance structure must include an independent oversight mechanism that assures compliance. The governance structure must also drive lessons learned back into the process, so the organization's risk management program minimally evolves at the same rate as the ever-changing threat and constantly changing market conditions. The control environment is the first line of defense against threat and vulnerabilities. The control environment must be continually reviewed in parallel with risk management activities to assure they are complementary and do not clash with one another. Before we get into the details of risk policy, governance, and control environment, we must first understand what we have to protect. The next several sections explore risk landscape, assets, threats, vulnerabilities, loss events, and risk scenarios.

Risk Landscape

Figure 20 depicts the overall risk landscape. The risk landscape consists of threats, threat events, and assets. The risk landscape includes many threats and threat events that are extremely unlikely to occur or can be effectively managed with internal controls. Assets are protected

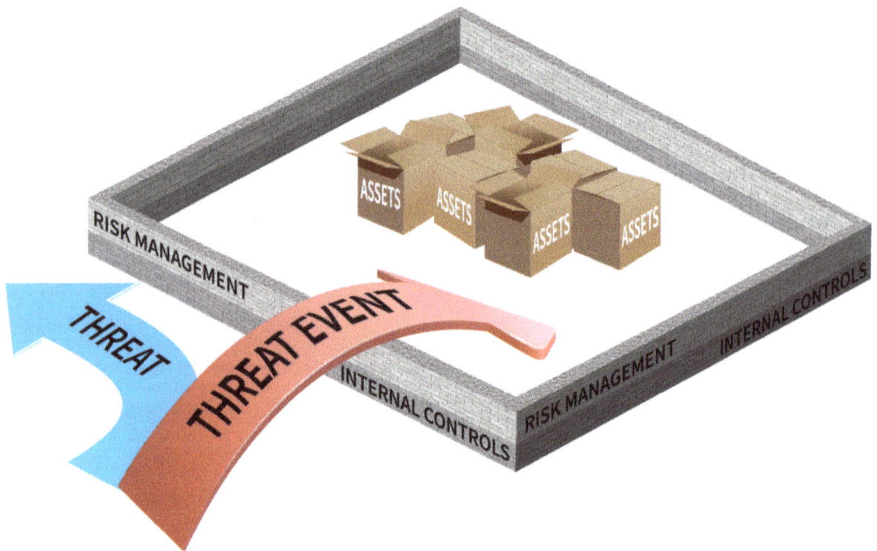

Figure 20: Risk Landscape

by a combination of risk management and <u>internal controls</u>. The key to effective risk management is to focus on those threats and threat events that can affect organizational assets and can be effectively managed with a combination of risk management and internal controls. Threats that won't realistically affect their assets often sidetrack many organizations. This asset-based approach is an excellent way to focus risk management, so risk practitioners and stakeholders are not distracted by threats and threat events that won't be able to exploit assets. For example, a public utility failure is a legitimate threat, but if the organization has a self-contained off-grid power system such as solar or wind generated power, then a utility failure will have little effect on organizational assets. In this example, the utility failure resides in the portion of the Threat Events box that is outside the risk management perimeter that protects organizational assets.

Assets

Assets are anything of value that is worth protecting and are used to meet goals and objectives. Assets can include facilities, equipment, software, intellectual property, customers, employees, reputation, data, and much more. An asset has four states in an asset-oriented risk management paradigm: low value, vulnerable and exploitable, vulnerable but not exploitable, and finally not vulnerable and not exploitable.

An asset that costs less than the cost to apply controls or mitigate residual risk characterizes the low-value state. One example of a low-value state is a lawn ornament purchased at a flea market for $1. The lawn ornament has monetary value as well as value in improving the appearance of the lawn; however, it would be fiscally irresponsible to spend elaborate sums to construct a security system to protect an asset worth $1. This asset state is very common, but many organizations fail to recognize cases where treatment cost exceeds the value of the asset, causing them to needlessly spend extraordinary sums of money and effort to protect the low value asset instead of simply replacing the asset for a fraction of the cost.

The vulnerable and exploitable state is characterized by an asset that is vulnerable and threats exist that can exploit the vulnerabilities. A car is a very simple example of an asset that is vulnerable and exploitable. A car is vulnerable if not locked, and simply locking the car door may not be sufficient to protect the asset from a theft risk event. Is an electronic security or theft deterrent system necessary to safeguard the car? This asset state is by far the most common, and it is where organizations should focus their risk management and internal control resources.

An asset having vulnerabilities that are potentially exploitable characterizes the vulnerable but not exploitable state, but there are no known threats that have the skill and motivation to exploit the vulnerabilities. The early iPhone is a good example of this state. Other manufacturer's smartphone vulnerabilities were exploited, but the iPhone appeared to be immune to similar threats because of their enhanced security features. This is a rather unusual asset state that is often overlooked. This asset state must be acknowledged and monitored because, just like the iPhone, it is only a matter of time before a threat agent comes along with the skills and motivation to exploit assets in this state.

The not vulnerable and not exploitable state is characterized by an asset that has known vulnerabilities but no known threats that are able to exploit the asset. The iPhone 5c is an example of the vulnerable and unexploitable state. The iPhone 5c was released in September 2013 and was considered unexploitable at the time. The iPhone 5c remained unexploited until April 2016 when the FBI announced that they paid professional hackers to break into a terrorist's phone. This is also a very unusual asset state and is associated with unique assets that are engineered to survive threats that are inconceivable at the time the asset is constructed. Be wary of this state because anything created by humans can eventually be exploited, it is just a matter of time.

Threats, Threat Agents, and Threat Events

Threats can include espionage, theft, software defects, mechanical failures, natural disasters, and much more. A threat event occurs when a threat agent uses a threat to exploit a vulnerability and acts against an asset such that its value to the organization is diminished. A threat event can only occur if there is a threat agent with the motivation and skill to exploit a vulnerability. A loss event occurs when a threat event exploits an asset's vulnerability and adversely affects the asset. A threat event can occur without having a loss event, but a loss event cannot occur without a threat event. *Figure 21* illustrates a stolen car threat event without a loss event. Car thieves (threats) seek to exploit vulnerabilities (unlocked car) to steal (threat event) cars (asset) but are apprehended in the act of stealing the car, therefore; a threat event occurs, but no loss event occurs.

Figure 21: Threat Event

Vulnerability

Vulnerabilities are weaknesses or gaps that present an opportunity for a threat to adversely impact an asset. An unlocked door is an example of a physical vulnerability to a facility. Network vulnerabilities include the absence of a firewall or an improperly configured firewall. Adding an internal control is the first step in treating vulnerabilities. Any remaining risk, after internal controls are applied, is managed through the risk management process.

Loss Events

A loss event is a risk event that occurs and results in a loss of use or impairment of assets. For a loss event to occur, a threat must act upon an asset such that loss results (The Open Group, 2014, p. 21). Using the car purchase referred to previously as an example, a stolen car results in a loss event associated with the car. The car thief is the threat, stolen car is the threat event, and losing the asset (e.g. car) is the loss event.

Risk Scenario

Risk scenario is a risk management technique contained in the Control Objectives for Information and Related Technology (COBIT) framework published by the Information Systems Audit and Control Association (ISACA). I have come to rely almost exclusively on risk scenarios as a way to describe risks because they more clearly describe the risk impact, and people seem more able to grasp the scenarios better than individual risk events.

A risk scenario, depicted in *Figure 22*, is an excellent way to conceptualize risk, which aids in the identification of threats and risk events. A risk scenario consists of five components; actor, threat type, risk event, asset,

RISK SCENARIO

ACTORS	THREAT TYPE		RISK EVENT		ASSETS	TIME
Internal	Malicious	Failure	Disclosure	Ineffective Design	People	Duration
External	Accidental	Nature	Interruption	Ineffective Execution	Org Structure	Timing
	External Requirement	Error	Modification	Rules & Regulations	Process	Detection
			Theft		Infastructure	Time Log
			Destruction	Inappropriate Use	Information	
					Applications	

Figure 22: Risk Scenario

and time. The actor in a risk scenario is the entity that generates the threat and may be internal actors or external actors. Keep in mind that the actor must have the skill and motivation (or access to assets in the case of internal actors) to exploit vulnerable assets. Some organizations waste valuable resources developing risk scenarios for actors with neither the motivation nor skill to exploit organizational assets.

The threat type is the nature of the threat event such as a malicious threat, an accidental threat, a failure threat, etc. The risk event is the event that can result in a loss affecting an organizational asset or objective. The asset is the entity that is affected by the risk event. Assets can include people (e.g. employees, customers, or suppliers), process assets, infrastructure, information, and more. Time is one of the more important elements of a risk scenario and consists of the duration of the risk event, the timing of the risk event, the time to detect the risk event, and time lag. We saw in previous case studies how timing and duration can dramatically affect the degree of impact associated with a loss event. The actors, threat types, risk events, assets and time elements are useful examples, to begin with. Over time an organization may expand on some or all of these scenario elements based on their industry, market conditions, and process maturity.

Those who are familiar with *Chaos to Clarity: The Tao of Risk Management* may recall the following syntax for concisely documenting a risk scenario. Recall the car theft example earlier in this chapter where a stolen car would affect our ability to meet our business objective of getting to work on time. Stating this situation in the form of a risk scenario allows the organization

<Actor> GENERATES <Threat> RESULTING IN <Event>
AFFECTING <Asset(s) / Resource(s)>
LEADING TO <business objective> <Impact><Time>

to look beyond the particular situation and start evaluating assets, threats, and risk events across the entire organization. It is now possible for risk managers to begin asking questions like, "How many people are affected by car theft?" The organization can now prepare a risk treatment plan to address unexpected late arrivals at an organizational level instead of many times at a project level as the various projects encounter the threat.

<Car Thief> GENERATES <Malicious Intent> RESULTING IN <Theft>
AFFECTING <Car>
LEADING TO <getting to work><Late><by 3 hours>

There are several advantages to this approach. First, it is more economical to fix a problem once instead of each time it occurs. Second, managing threats and risk events at an organizational level allows later projects to alter their approach and avoid any impact altogether instead of mitigating the risk event to minimize the impact as the threat or risk event is recognized. Finally, managing threats and risk events at an organizational level reduces the overall exposure caused by inexperienced or less skilled resources.

Risk Policy

The organization's risk policy is the foundation upon which the risk management program is built. I like to focus on the essential elements of risk management that result in effective risk management. To that end, I reviewed numerous sources of risk management guidance and settled on three international risk management standards; ISO 31000 Risk management — Principles and guidelines, ISO 16085 Systems and software engineering — Lifecycle processes — Risk Management, and the Australian / New Zealand Risk Management Standard AN/NZS 4360. AN/NZS 4360 has been subsumed by other standards and subsequently discontinued. However, I still find it to be an excellent reference because it contains more detail and better examples than current standards. These three standards have a consistent view of what a risk policy should contain. There are seven common elements these three standards suggest should be addressed in a risk policy:

- State the organization's objectives for managing risk

- Clearly state the organization's commitment to manage risk

- Describe the rationale for managing risk

- Explicitly link organizational objectives with risk policy

- Resources are made available to manage risk

- How risk information is reported and communicated

- A commitment to formally review and improve the risk policy on a periodic basis

Five of the seven items noted above are pretty standard for an organizational policy of any type. Explicitly linking organizational objectives to the risk policy and describing how risk information is reported are two of the most important elements of risk policy. Linking organizational objectives to the risk policy makes it easy to communicate risk impact to stakeholders and clearly demonstrates the organization's commitment to managing risk. Without a consistent and effective communication mechanism, the risk management program will rapidly deteriorate.

Quantitative versus Qualitative Measures

I strongly advocate using quantitative measures for risk. Many people disagree with using quantitative risk measures giving the excuse that risk is all about uncertainty, so qualitative measures are more appropriate. I contend that being unable to clearly state the risk impact in a quantitative manner indicates that the risk assessment and subsequent risk analysis is insufficient and/or incomplete. Countless tools and techniques allow risk practitioners to establish quantitative risk impact and treatment cost especially if organizational objectives are mapped to the risk policy. *ISO 31010 Risk management – Risk assessment techniques* describes 31 risk assessment techniques that enable risk practitioners to drive out quite a lot of uncertainty and derive a reasonably accurate range which is much better than simply stating the risk impact in qualitative terms.

Factor Analysis of Information Risk (FAIR) is another excellent technique for establishing quantitative risk impact. FAIR provides a taxonomy and method for understanding, analyzing, and measuring information risk (The Open Group, 2014). One of the greatest benefits of FAIR is that it allows organizations to view their risk in totality including vulnerabilities, loss event frequency, loss event magnitude, threat capabilities, and much more.

Quantitative Appetite and Tolerance

Explicitly stating the organization's risk appetite and risk tolerance in quantitative terms is an excellent way to document risk management objectives, facilitate linking organizational objectives to the risk policy, and simplify risk reporting. Documenting quantitative risk appetite and risk tolerance in the risk policy makes the appetite and tolerance thresholds very clear.

I conducted a series of informal polls in preparation for speaking at an international risk management conference. I surveyed a number of random people, some who had risk management backgrounds and others who did not. The first question I asked was, "What is a high budget amount?" The second question I asked was, "What is a long duration?"

The answers to the budget question ranged from $3.5 million to $1 trillion. The answers to the duration question ranged from five years to 50 years. What is high or low depends on someone's role in the organization and their level of experience. This example clearly illustrates why qualitative risk measures and thresholds can be very problematic.

The University of Edinburgh in Edinburgh, Scotland publishes their risk policy online. The university's risk policy provides a good example of quantitatively documenting their risk appetite and tolerance for financial risk and education and student experience. The risk policy provides six quantitative values for measuring and controlling financial risk. Two examples are, 1) ensure long-term borrowings never exceed 20% of net assets and 2) ensure that at least three months equivalent spending is held in cash or cash equivalents or in negotiated bank facilities. In this case, the tolerance and thresholds are very clear and cannot be misinterpreted.

Risk Appetite and Context

There are two aspects of risk appetite that must be considered when expressing risk appetite in quantitative terms. First, there will likely be an organizational appetite to consider such as "Risk appetite for budget risk can not exceed 20% of net assets." Second, the organization may want to consider establishing a risk appetite for individual projects, initiatives, divisions, etc. *Figure 23* includes examples of quantitative measures that can be used to express risk impact. An example of safety risk appetite could be, "Risk appetite for safety risk must be no more than 20 lost work days per calendar quarter." Organizational appetite examples are, "Division budget risk can not exceed a total of $1 million."

The risk policy should explicitly state appetite thresholds for each of the six context elements; schedule risk, budget risk, quality risk, mission risk, safety risk, and reputation risk.

RISK CONTEXT	EXAMPLE MEASURES
SCHEDULE RISK	Days, weeks, months, years
BUDGET RISK	Currency
QUALITY RISK	Defect density, warranty claims
MISSION RISK	Organizational objectives not achieved
SAFETY RISK	Loss of life, lost work days from injury
REPUTATION RISK	Customer satisfaction ratings, focus group results, independent assessment results

Figure 23: Quantitative Measure Examples

Governance

Governance, oversight, and risk tolerance are tightly interwoven and are critical to effectively implementing a risk policy. Good governance is transparent, provides accountability, is lawful, responsive to the needs of the organization, equitable, and effective. Governance is a set of processes for making and implementing decisions. Governance is not about making the correct decision but more about making the best decision based on the available information.

Risk governance begins with the risk policy, which enforces accountability and lawfulness. The risk management plans and processes are then used to implement the risk policy and provide transparency. The control environment and performance reporting provide stakeholders the information they need to adapt to the changing needs of the organization. Performance reporting also assures the governance processes are equitable across the organization and enables effective risk management.

Flexibility is one of the most important aspects of risk governance.

Globalization drives innovation at a frenetic pace causing organizations to be in a constant state of change so they can maintain their competitive edge and combat rapidly evolving threats. There can be cases where a company division wants to charter a project or enter into a new business venture that comes with $1 million worth of budget risk, but the organization has already reached its appetite limit for budget risk. The governance and oversight functions must recognize that even though the divisional appetite is at or below the established threshold, it may not be possible to charter the new venture because the organization is at or above the published budget appetite threshold.

The organizational risk tolerance should be defined in such a manner that stakeholders and decision makers can make quick decisions. For example, an organization may temporarily authorize an initiative to continue through the initiation phase so that additional information can be gathered and offer an opportunity to potentially mitigate a sufficient amount of budget risk so the initiative can proceed. It is also possible that the organization's risk posture will change in the near future or that the organization may choose to increase its risk appetite. In this example, the risk tolerance could be defined as "budget risk can exceed the published appetite threshold by no more than 5% for a period no longer than four months."

Link Risk to Organizational Objectives

Risk scenarios are an excellent way to link organizational objectives to high-impact risk events. A series of risk scenarios for each of the risk context elements enables the organization to clearly understand to what extent potential risk events can impact organizational objectives and assets. Identifying high-impact risk events at the organizational level allows stakeholders and decision makers to more effectively manage risk impact and meet strategic business objectives.

Conducting regular risk and control environment assessments is a good way to proactively identify new and emerging threats. Evaluating risk scenarios during these assessments helps facilitate rapid response to new threats and allows the organization to quickly develop deterrent and compensating controls to reduce the likelihood that a new threat can exploit known vulnerabilities.

Roles and Responsibilities

Clearly defining roles, responsibilities, and explicit risk ownership is essential to effective risk management. This section of the risk policy is where an organization can describe whether they have a risk committee, a risk review board, or some other way to adjudicate risk items and advise senior management. It is also critical in this section to explicitly identify risk owners. Many organizations tend to push risk ownership to low levels within the organization, which can be problematic. Recall the risk ownership discussion earlier where the risk owner is the individual or single role that owns the assets affected by a loss event. This is the section of the risk policy where the board of directors, or equivalent, can clearly establish accountability for risk management. Keeping in mind that risk owners must be able to commit

RISK CONTEXT	OWNER
SCHEDULE RISK	Chief Operations Officer (COO)
BUDGET RISK	Chief Financial Officer (CFO)
QUALITY RISK	Chief Quality Officer (CQO)
MISSION RISK	Chief Executive Officer (CEO)
SAFETY RISK	Chief Operations Officer (COO)
REPUTATION RISK	Chairman of the Board

Figure 24: Risk Context and Ownership

strategic resources to manage and treat risk events, it stands to reason that risk owners should be board members and senior executives. *Figure 24* illustrates one example of how risk ownership can be aligned by risk context. Aligning risk owners with six risk context elements described earlier draws a consistent thread throughout the entire risk policy.

Performance Measures

A Key Performance Indicator (KPI) is used to measure process performance and maturity and to assure that organizational goals are met. A Key Risk Indicator (KRI) is a leading indicator that provides an early warning mechanism thereby allowing an organization to proactively take action so the KPI can be met even though a problem has been encountered. Understanding that KPIs are retrospective and KRIs are forward-looking is critical to creating effective KPIs and KRIs.

KPIs should be used to measure things such as how complete information is, information timeliness, process compliance, and information accuracy. KPIs must also include elements of process improvement and an active feedback loop. An active feedback loop consists of organizational processes that not only drive collection of improvement recommendations and lessons learned but also drives process modifications to prevent recurrence of undesirable outcomes or behaviors.

A passive feedback loop is a major failure point for an organization. A passive feedback loop consists of organizational processes that collect improvement recommendations and lessons learned and then store them in a repository. The primary failure of passive feedback is that it relies on individual behavior and organizational culture that prioritizes process improvement ahead of schedules. The current global economy seems to drive constant schedule pressure regardless of the industry, so a passive feedback loop is very problematic even in highly process mature organizations such as CMMI Level 5 organizations.

KRI information is typically based on trend analysis and data correlation. Many organizations confuse KPIs and KRIs and end up creating process measures but calling them KRIs. KRIs should be forward-looking and provide enough information that decision makers can make an informed decision that enables the organization to reduce their risk.

Let's consider a simplistic example to help illustrate the point. We want to take a road trip across the country. The trip is 3,600 miles long (1,800 miles each way), we plan to drive a leisurely 350 miles per day, our car averages 32 miles per gallon (mpg), and, we estimate the average fuel price to be $2.35 per gallon. Based on these parameters our trip will take slightly more than ten days, consume 112.5 gallons of gas and cost $264.38. To allow for price fluctuations, we budget $275 for fuel.

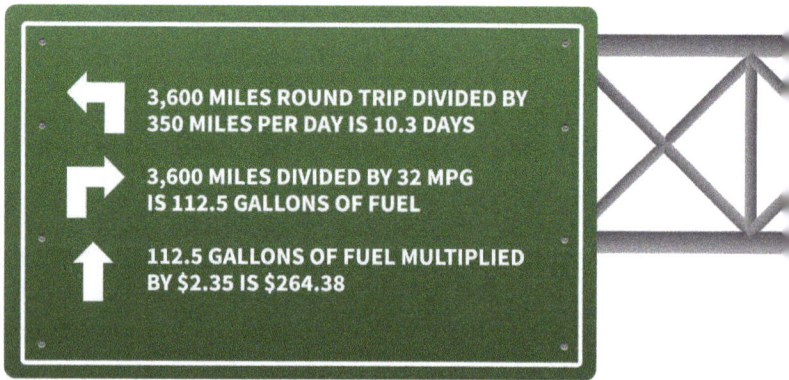

Figure 25: Road Trip Calculations

The KPI, in this case, is "Projects Completed Within Budget." Waiting until the end of the project to measure success eliminates any opportunity to meet the KPI if any risk events are encountered along the way. One way to make sure we stay on budget is to monitor fuel consumption and fuel expenditures along the way. Monitoring fuel consumption and fuel expenditures is an example of a KRI because it provides the ability to measure current progress against the original plan and predict whether fuel consumption and the associated budget will exceed the original estimate.

When defining KPIs or KRIs, it is important that process documentation describes at a minimum how information is captured, where information is stored, how information is reported, the data owner, and who information is reported to. Some organizations may require many more details, but this is the basic set of information that should satisfy most needs.

Anyone who has ever been on a long road trip knows that gas prices and vehicle mileage vary with location, weather, and terrain. There are at least a couple risk events associated with increased gas prices and worse than expected mileage. For the sake of this exercise let's establish one KRI to monitor fuel consumption and another KRI to measure mileage. To stay on budget (the stated KPI), the travelers will need to capture and report fuel consumption measurements on a daily basis.

The travelers monitor mileage throughout the first day of the trip and find that the average mileage is two mpg less than expected and the average fuel price is ten cents a gallon more than was estimated. In this case, we see that the mileage is less than anticipated, so there are few options at this point. The trip can be re-planned for a shorter trip, the travelers can continue for another day or two to see if mileage improves, or the travelers can compute the estimate fuel consumption to determine whether the $15 fuel contingency is enough to offset the lower mileage. Recalculating the fuel cost at 30 mpg and $2.45 per gallon reveals that the estimated cost will be $294, which clearly exceeds the planned budget leaving two options to consider, re-plan or continue to see if the situation improves. The organizational risk appetite and tolerance would inform the next decision point. A risk-averse organization would likely re-plan the trip to stay within budget and compromise the business objective. Conversely, companies with higher risk appetite or risk tolerance would likely continue for a few more days to see if the conditions improve or get worse.

We can continue to work through more scenarios as we continue with the road trip but this initial exercise serves to illustrate the point that KRIs provide the ability to predict probable outcomes based on data that is collected. The key point here is that KPIs and KRIs go hand in hand. One without the other doesn't help much except to demonstrate that data can be collected and reported. One must have a process in place to collect meaningful data, and data that is collected must have predictive elements that are germane to the objective.

Now let's take the road trip a little bit further. Our trip was estimated to take slightly more than ten days, consume 112.5 gallons of gas and cost $264.38. Our business objective is to complete the road trip within ten days and spend less than $275 on fuel. The business objective contains two elements: duration, and budget. For simplicity's sake, we will ignore the duration element for now and focus on the budget element. The risk statements for the budget element are:

IF fuel prices increase more than 9 cents THEN, the project budget is insufficient to complete road trip

IF car mileage is less than 30.8 mpg THEN, the project budget is insufficient to complete road trip

Recall that the business objective is to complete all projects within budget. The KPI measures the number of projects completed within budget. To meet the business objective and satisfy KPI, the travelers establish a KRI to monitor their mileage throughout the trip. At the end of the first day, the travelers find that the average mileage was two mpg less than planned and the average fuel price was ten cents a gallon more than was estimated. At this point, the travelers know they will consume 120 gallons of fuel (7.5 gallons more than planned) and spend $294 ($29.62 more than expected, and $19 more than the contingency budget). Since budget is the business driver, the travelers would focus on the fuel cost and recalculate the trip mileage, and duration. Remember the original trip objectives were to cover 3,600 miles in 10.3 days, consume 112.5 gallons of fuel, and spend less than $275. Re-planning the trip using the KRI data reveals that the travelers can achieve three of the four original objectives by reducing the trip distance from 3,600 to 3,367 miles.

The 3,367-mile trip can be completed in 9.6 days, consume 112.2 gallons of fuel, and not exceed the $275 fuel budget.

Governance, Oversight, and Assurance

The risk management process is not complicated, but executing the process correctly can be very difficult. For risk management to be effective, the process must be enforced at both the tactical and strategic level. Effective oversight of the tactical risk management process can be provided by a combination of quality assurance reviews and management reviews. Oversight of the strategic risk management process requires an effective governance process consisting of a risk policy, risk management plans, and a risk adjudication mechanism. Without adequate oversight, the effectiveness of organizational risk management can quickly deteriorate due in large part to the challenging nature of risk management.

While management consists of actual decisions made, governance offers a structure for making those decisions. It is critical for organizations to establish a governance structure so executive sponsors can steer the organization as necessary, and the more tactical business and technical personnel can continue with the day to day development of effective results.

The role of governance is to offer a decision-making mechanism that consists of policy makers, committees, and adjudication boards. An executive steering committee (ESC) typically focuses on strategy, investment, and architecture. The ESC also has a responsibility to assign the decision-making authority and accountability. Compliance monitoring provides oversight to assure policy compliance. Adjudication boards represent the next level of governance to assure performance. Committees are constituted as needed to collect information, perform analysis of alternatives, and survey stakeholders so recommendations can be presented to the ESC for consideration and action.

The risk profile is a critical part of the governance process. The risk profile is based on the overall risk posture of the organization reflected in its attentiveness in monitoring the effectiveness of controls, proactivity in identifying and addressing or preventing risk and development of a risk culture (ISACA, 2015, p. 163). The risk profile is the reflection of risk that exists at all levels of the organization. Like safety risk, the cascading effects of many minor risk events can affect the risk posture of the entire organization. The risk profile must be reviewed and updated on a continuous basis as new threats emerge, new vulnerabilities are discovered, regulations change, morale in the organization changes, market conditions change, or any other condition that affects the organization's assets.

Governance provides the framework, principles, structure, processes and practices to set direction, monitor compliance, and assure performance. Setting direction ensures that stakeholder needs, conditions, and options are evaluated so agreed-upon enterprise objectives can be achieved through disciplined prioritization and decision making. Advisory groups can be formed to study particular problems and formulate recommendations to the ESC. Defining the organizational risk policy is one risk governance function performed by the ESC.

The Program Management Office's (PMO) Quality Management function often performs compliance monitoring; it also assures policy. Compliance monitoring includes metrics management, Service Level Agreement (SLA) reporting, trend analysis, risk modeling, variance analysis, process audits, and root cause analysis (RCA). Enterprise goal alignment is a function of compliance monitoring and includes project management oversight, enterprise-wide change management oversight, enterprise-wide issue management, and enterprise risk management. Risk management is critical to enterprise goal alignment.

An effective risk management program provides information to senior leadership so risks can be treated promptly to minimize the impact to enterprise goals and objectives. An Enterprise Risk Policy is the most important critical success factor. It must include risk appetite and risk tolerance thresholds. The Enterprise Risk Policy establishes the foundation for the Enterprise Risk Management Plan (E-RMP), the Risk Review Board (RRB), and Project Risk Management Plans (P-RMP).

The **E-RMP** establishes a process to manage enterprise risks and includes reporting to senior leadership.
P-RMPs establish individual project processes for identifying and reporting project risks. Project risks are submitted to the RRB for consideration to be managed at the enterprise level.
The **RRB** performs risk reviews to understand and approve risks, evaluate those risks against the costs required to mitigate them, and direct or approve the risk handling approaches and risk mitigation activities (e.g., Risk Mitigation Plan, Contingency Plan). The goal of the RRB is to assess risks for completeness and consistency and provide communication of the risks to all stakeholders. The RRB initially reviews and approves the foundational elements of the risk management program including risk policy, governance structure, risk assessment practices, risk management practices, guidelines, and processes for managing, treating and reporting risks. After approval of the risk management program, the RRB reviews candidate risks on a regular basis (typically monthly) to classify risks, assign risk parameters, approve treatment plans, and continuously evaluate risks.

Governance is about negotiating and deciding amongst different stakeholders' value interests. Consequently, the governance system should consider all stakeholders when making benefit, risk, and resource assessment decisions. For each decision, three questions should be asked: For whom are the benefits? Who bears the risk? What resources are required?

Advisory groups can be formed in addition to committees to consider alternatives for satisfying stakeholder needs, quantifying benefits, assessing risk, etc.

Feedback Loop

An active feedback loop is one area where an organization can derive tremendous value from risk management. One characteristic of active feedback loops is a defined process that continuously pushes information throughout the organization. Information must be actively and continuously driven while lessons learned and risk models are developed or modified. Waiting until lessons learned and risk models are "done" is a losing battle. The rapid pace of market changes in today's global economy causes information to quickly stagnate. Lessons learned quickly become obsolete if they do not evolve as fast, or faster than, today's dynamic global environment. Actively disseminating information allows project teams to leverage enhanced risk models, lessons learned, and best practices on a near real-time basis. Wiki, or other collaboration software, are excellent tools for providing active feedback to project teams, especially distributed teams because it drives active participation in the data collection and dissemination processes.

Control Environment

An effective control environment is one of the most important aspects of risk management and is often neglected. Risk practitioners often overlook organizational controls because they are perceived to belong to the audit or compliance part of the organization. Effective risk management programs tightly integrate the control environment with ERM activities.

Controls are focused on assets that are vulnerable to a threat. A control assessment or risk assessment must seek to identify assets that have vulnerabilities. Vulnerabilities must then be analyzed to determine whether there are threat agents with the motivation and skill to exploit the vulnerability. If a control or risk assessment determines that vulnerabilities exist, and there are threat agents with the motivation and ability to exploit the vulnerability, then a risk event exists. If the threat agent(s) act upon the asset then a threat event exists. The first step to managing the risk event is to determine whether the organization can implement a control to protect the asset. If a control can protect the asset, then the risk impact will likely be low. This risk event should be added to the risk register with a strategy to mitigate, with the risk treatment specifying the control that was implemented. Even though a control has been implemented to mitigate the risk event, there may be residual or secondary risk that requires further treatment and monitoring.

Controls come in two forms: proactive and reactive. Proactive controls are also referred to as safeguards, and reactive controls are also known as countermeasures. Proactive controls include four categories of controls: compensating controls, deterrent controls, directive controls, and preventive controls. Reactive controls include two categories of controls: corrective controls and detective controls.

Compensating controls are used to neutralize known deficiencies. Compensating controls seek to reduce the likelihood that a threat event can exploit an asset's vulnerability. Two-factor authentication for computer login is an example of a compensating control that mitigates poor password policies and users who use weak passwords.

Deterrent controls use warnings or banners to deter threat agents. Deterrent controls seek to reduce the likelihood that a threat agent will attempt to exploit an asset's vulnerability. Warnings include things such as "This area under video surveillance." Banners include splash screens such as

You are entering an Official United States Government System that may be used only by authorized users for authorized purposes. Unauthorized access is a violation of the laws of the U.S. and may result in administrative or criminal penalties.

Directive controls direct the behavior of people using the asset. Directive controls seek to reduce asset vulnerability. Policies, budget limits, and system configurations are examples of directive controls.

Preventive controls inhibit threat agents from exploiting vulnerabilities.

Preventive controls seek to protect the asset from exploitation and reduce the impact if an asset's vulnerability is exploited by a threat event. Data encryption is an example of a preventive control for an IT system. A security fence is an example of a preventive control for a physical asset.

Corrective controls are implemented during or after an asset's vulnerability is exploited by a threat event. Corrective controls seek to decrease the impact of the threat event. A business continuity plan is one example of a corrective control. Automatic sprinklers are another corrective control example for a physical asset.

Detective controls are used to discover violations, attempted violations, or instances of threat events. Detective controls seek to prevent an asset's vulnerabilities from being exploited, reduce the impact of threat events, and often trigger the development and implementation of preventive controls. Audits and system logs are examples of detective controls.

Bidirectional traceability of controls, vulnerabilities, threat events, and risk events are critical for effective risk management. Risk assessments must seek to continuously verify and validate the control environment and assure full traceability. Obsolete controls can consume critical resources and falsely report asset vulnerabilities, so it is imperative that the control environment is comprehensively reviewed on a regular basis. Conversely, inadequate controls can allow vulnerabilities to be exploited and go unreported for quite some time. A recent example of an extended exploited vulnerability is the Democratic National Committee (DNC) data breach by Russian hackers in June 2016. Russian hackers were able to access the DNC computer system for over a year before they were detected (Nakashima, 2016, p. 1).

CHAPTER 7

SPOT AND AVOID RISK PITFALLS

Spot Risk Pitfalls

This chapter summarizes four organizational culture characteristics from the previous case studies. Gone unchecked, these characteristics can yield catastrophic results. This chapter offers leading indicators of impending disaster that risk practitioners must be on the lookout for. I must point out that this is not an exhaustive list of leading indicators nor do the presence of these leading indicators mean that disaster is imminent. However, the presence of any of these leading indicators is certainly cause for concern and warrants a serious discussion with the risk management organization.

Profit Above all Else

As we have seen in the GM, Toyota, and BP case studies, organizations that allow profits to overshadow safety risk and sound risk management practices are on a path to disaster. Unfortunately, the path to disaster can be quite long, which exponentially increases the overall loss event impact. Situations such as these can be compounded by a series of near misses that the organization is seemingly able to avoid giving rise to normalized deviance. Eventually, the near misses add up, and the final impact can be quite significant. The laser-like focus on profits combined with a series of near misses and normalized deviance results in loss of life, billions of dollars in financial impact, and untold damage to the company's reputation.

There are three leading indicators to be on the lookout for: culture that drives people to emphasize profits over safety and reputation risk, near misses that are tolerated and not corrected, and normalized deviance.

Rejection and Deception

Organizations suppress critical information for a variety of reasons. As we saw in the GM and Toyota case studies, information was concealed or ignored to contain cost and maximize profits. Conventional wisdom seems to indicate that VW knew about the defeat device on diesel vehicles and used that as a means to grow market share. Investigations are ongoing at VW, so the jury is still out about whether they knowingly installed the defeat device software on diesel vehicles or the software was installed by mistake and not removed once they realized the effect. We also saw a case where risk entries were converted to opportunities as a way to escape risk discussions during management reviews.

In all four cases,there were individuals who reported these issues to management but the organizational culture allowed managers to ignore the warnings and proceed. In some cases, the results can be relatively benign by simply allowing someone to avoid embarrassing or uncomfortable situations. In other cases, the deception and cover-up led to loss of life and billions of dollars in financial impact.

We saw one case where an organization constructed a rather elaborate risk management Potemkin Village. Potemkin Villages indirectly affect organizational objectives by wasting significant amounts of time and money. The culture that spawns Potemkin Villages and allows them to flourish is the real danger.

Be wary of situations where there seems to a flurry of activity but no real progress. Lots of activity with little to no progress is one warning sign of a Potemkin Village. This situation can be compounded by individuals who have a vested interest in maintaining the façade of the Potemkin Village.

Years ago I worked with an organization that was being pressured by corporate executives to improve product quality and process compliance. Driven by corporate pressure, divisional executives launched a quality improvement program. The division charted a quality initiative to achieve a Capability Maturity Model (CMM) level 3. CMM was the predecessor to the current Capability Maturity Model – Integrated (CMMI) that was originally sponsored by the Software Engineering Institute (SEI) at Carnegie Mellon University.

The division charted the quality improvement initiative, staffed the initiative, created plans, conducted meetings, and expended a great deal of effort. While there was lots of activity, there was very little progress. To make a long story short, the organization launched this same quality initiative five different times. There always seemed to be some critical need that arose six months or so into the quality improvement initiative that caused resources to be reassigned and the initiative was tabled for several months. This scenario played out time after time for about ten years until there was a divisional leadership change. With new leadership, the organization was able to achieve the CMMI Level 3 goal in less than 18 months. Think what could have been accomplished with all the wasted effort and lost productivity over the course of a decade! In addition to the raw cost of building and maintaining a Potemkin Village, there are also intangible costs including lost opportunities and low employee morale.

We saw two examples in the governmental agency where stakeholders were presented with quantitative information from multiple sources, yet they refused to accept the data. This is clearly an example of people simply not wanting to act on the data, which is akin to simply sticking your head in the sand. People who continuously ask for more data or more detail is another characteristic of an organization or individual who does not want to act on the data; the only difference is that their approach is proactive instead of passively ignoring data. Both cases doom the organization to incur all risk because the default treatment strategy is acceptance.

Avoid Risk Pitfalls

Three techniques can be used to help spot and avoid risk management pitfalls: pulling the thread, risk assessments, and KRIs.

The first strategy, what I call "pulling the thread," is exactly what you expect it to be. If you keep pulling on the loose thread in a sweater, you eventually get to the other end. The same concept applies here. When you see something that doesn't quite make sense, pull on the thread. Keep pulling and asking questions until you get to the end and confirm whether or not there is a problem.

Let's examine the risk management Potemkin Village to help illustrate how this works in practice. We know that effective risk management includes a risk policy, governance, risk management plans, internal controls, and risk reporting. In a reasonably well-managed risk management program you should be able to follow the thread from the risk policy through the risk management plans, the governance process, the internal controls, and ultimately to the lowest level of reporting, which in most cases is the risk register. The key is to be able to follow the thread from the topmost policy to the lowest level of reporting. Any lack of traceability from policy to the lowest level process indicates potential gaps that require further investigation. Pulling the thread is an excellent way to detect the presence of profits above all else, deception and cover-up, and Potemkin Villages. Process audits, product assessments, and evaluations are excellent ways to initiate pulling the thread.

A risk assessment is an excellent way to identify cases where an organization is sticking their head in the sand. ISO 31010 is an international standard that describes risk assessment techniques. ISO 31010 has a very well-defined risk assessment process including controls assessment. The standard also describes 31 different risk assessment techniques that apply to all industries. A risk assessment is an excellent technique to use when encountering gaps or anomalies when pulling the thread. A risk assessment can also highlight entities within an organization that are sticking their head in the sand.

The Orange Book establishes three risk assessment principles. The first principle is to ensure that there is a clearly structured process for evaluating the likelihood and impact for each risk. The second principle is to record the results of the risk assessment in a manner that facilitates monitoring and identification of risk priorities. The third principle emphasizes the need to clearly articulate the differences between inherent and residual risk after controls are applied (riskAC). Inherent risk is risk that exists before implementing any internal controls or risk management. RiskAC is risk that remains after implementing internal controls. The risk profile is a primary output of the risk assessment process.

KRIs are excellent indicators of potential problems. However, KRIs must be properly defined to be effective. Organizations frequently make two common mistakes when defining KRIs. The first mistake is to define too many KRIs and the second mistake is to confuse KRIs with KPIs. ISACA offers the SMART methodology for defining KRIs. SMART stands for Specific, Measurable, Attainable, Relevant, and Timely (ISACA, 2015, p. 154). A KRI must be:

- **S**pecific to a clearly understood organizational goal
- **M**easured in quantitative, not qualitative, terms
- **A**ttainable and realistic
- **R**elevant to the specific activity or goal
- **T**imely so corrective action can be implemented

The quantitative nature of a KRI makes them invaluable for identifying Potemkin Villages and cover-ups. The alignment with organizational goals and quantitative measures also make KRIs useful for corroborating the results of audits, assessments, and evaluations.

I have seen many organizations collect and report on countless data elements that are completely irrelevant to meeting organizational objectives. Simply being able to collect and report data does not necessarily mean that you can create KPIs or KRIs. Many organizations struggle to create KPIs and KRIs, so they resort to "start by reporting what we have." Instead, you must begin by asking, "How do we know we are meeting organizational objectives?" Trying to craft KPIs and KRIs based on data that is already being collected can be a bit problematic because the focus becomes the data and reporting mechanism instead of the organizational objective.

Ishaq Bhatti examined 84 of the best manufacturing organizations in Pakistan and found that key performance indicators (KPI) could be placed into one of 11 categories (Ishaq Bhatti, 2014). The KPIs are consistent with many industries other than just manufacturing. Further analysis of these KPIs indicates that several of them are subsets of six larger categories: schedule, budget, quality, safety, delivery reliability, and reputation. These six KPIs form the basis of organizational performance and context elements for ERM.

The key is to develop companion KRIs for these six KPIs. KRIs and KPIs that are properly paired give organizations time to implement corrective action so risk impact can be minimized and organizational objectives can be achieved. Consider an organization that has an organizational goal of completing all projects on time. To meet the organizational goal, a schedule KPI is established that requires project managers to report schedule information on a weekly basis and reconcile actual progress and expenditures with the baseline estimates.

This schedule KPI could be paired with KRIs based on the schedule performance index (SPI). SPI is a performance measure that project managers use to measure the degree of variance from the schedule baseline. An SPI of 1.0 indicates that there is no variance between the current schedule and baseline schedule. An SPI less than 1.0 indicates the project is behind schedule (e.g. less work was completed than planned) and an SPI greater than 1.0 indicates the project is ahead of schedule (e.g. more work was completed than was planned).

Two KRIs can be established for the SPI. KRI #1 could be an SPI value of 0.9 and KRI #2 could be a declining SPI for three consecutive reporting periods (e.g. Week 1 – SPI 0.99, Week 2 – SPI 0.98, Week 3 – SPI 0.97). Both KRIs align with ISACA SMART methodology; both KRIs are 1) specific and directly align with the organizational schedule goal, 2) quantitative (measurable), 3) attainable (SPI of 0.9 is a common threshold used in many industries), 4) relevant to the organizational goal and the schedule KPI, and 5) timely. KRI #2 indicates an undesirable trend is developing and allows correct action to be taken even before the SPI 0.9 threshold is reached.

CHAPTER 8

CARE AND FEEDING OF ORGANIZATIONAL CULTURE

Organizational Culture

Organizational culture, if carefully nurtured, can be the organization's most valuable asset. However, organizational culture unchecked by effective risk management can yield disastrous results as we have seen in the GM, Toyota, and VW case studies. Organizational culture can't be legislated or dictated, it is a reflection of the deep-rooted beliefs of senior management. Senior management must unequivocally instill and reinforce their beliefs every day. Even a single lapse can open a hairline crack that quickly becomes a chasm impossible to bridge. Research into risk management disasters points to organizational culture as the key failure point when cultural collapse occurs. Organizational culture is the key element that allows organizations to survive cultural collapse and reestablish themselves after a disaster.

In reviewing the organizational culture at Keane and HP, we saw how enduring it can be yet fragile at the same time. As we saw in the case of Keane and HP, organizational culture allows the organization to navigate any manner of market disasters over many decades, but once the organizational culture is destroyed it is nearly impossible to reestablish.

HP's organizational culture allowed them to successfully navigate 60 years of some of the greatest technological changes of the 20th Century. A single precipitating event destroyed the culture in a matter of months, and now, more than 16 years later, HP is still struggling to reestablish their organizational culture and even their commercial viability. A key observation from Keane and HP is that in both cases the company founders ran the company for more than 40 years, which is markedly different than the average tenure of CEOs today. According to Fortune Magazine, the average tenure of Fortune 500 Company CEOs in 2015 was 6.9 years (DeCarlo & VanderMey, 2015).

According to Don MacPherson, it takes three years to change the organizational culture for medium to large organizations (MacPherson, 2014). It generally takes a new incoming CEO nearly a year to get fully integrated into the organization. A culture change initiative will take many months of planning and several more months to launch the initiative. By this time we are at least two years into the CEO's tenure leaving very little time to implement the initiative before the CEO is likely to leave the organization. Organizational culture requires organizational values and beliefs to be consistently reinforced in order to survive. The CEO revolving door does not provide a stable enough environment for organizational culture to thrive. Thus, organizations should consider moving responsibility for organizational culture to the board of directors.

Risk Culture

We explored 136 years of organizational culture and risk management failures throughout the course of *Cultural Calamity*. Lowell Carr researched disasters from 1881 to 1928 and concluded that all disasters follow a consistent pattern driven in large part by regional and organizational culture. Forty-four years later, in 1976, Barry Turner researched a series of disasters in Great Britain. Turner states that a disaster or cultural collapse occurs because of an inaccuracy or inadequacy in accepted norms and beliefs (Turner, 1976). The case studies we explored in Chapter Four exhibited cultural failures consistent with Turner's conclusions 44 years prior and Carr's conclusions 84 years prior. HP's history clearly shows that organizational culture allows organizations to successfully navigate very challenging market conditions. Unfortunately, the HP story also shows how difficult it is for an organization to recover from a cultural collapse.

Enhance your risk culture by embracing the basic tenets of HROs. Become preoccupied by failure, reject the premise that simplified interpretations benefit the organization, inject operational sensitivity into the organizational culture, commit to organizational resilience, and consider flexible organizational structures that can swiftly adapt to urgent or crisis situations.

The preoccupation with failure allows organizations to avoid normalized deviance. Organizations preoccupied by failure tend to seek quantitative data so detailed analysis can be conducted. Analysis confirms the presence of threats and vulnerabilities as well as the associated impact on organizational assets so the corresponding risk events can be effectively managed.

The reluctance to simplify interpretations allows organizations to avoid problems caused by normalizing risk for reporting purposes. The desire for quantitative data instead of simplifying the interpretation of data is the basis for a highly effective risk management program and facilitates the seamless integration of risk governance and process improvement. Had GM and BP been sensitive to operational situations instead of being laser focused on revenue and profits, they could have avoided the multi-billion dollar loss events and loss of life associated with the ignition switch debacle and Macondo oil spill respectively. Had BP been committed to resilience and a more flexible structure that allowed operational personnel to make decisions, the effects of the Macondo well disaster would likely have been less severe.

Organizations that support flexible organizational structures can benefit greatly from a risk management organization that has an independent reporting path to the topmost stakeholder(s). This independent reporting path is one way to effectively combat the many risk management challenges presented throughout *Cultural Calamity*.

Risk practitioners must be constantly vigilant for signs of a risk hurricane. Risk hurricanes, if allowed to persist, can erode organizational culture, leading to cultural collapse over time. The tenets of HRO, collective learning, and asset-based risk management provide some of the best defense against a risk hurricane. Don't allow yourself or your organization to fall prey to normalized deviance, risk normalization, rejection, or deception. Be skeptical, look forward but keep an eye on lessons of the past, and always challenge the status quo. Most important of all, recognize the value of organizational culture, understand that it can be easily destroyed, and that reestablishing organizational culture after a collapse can be a monumental effort.

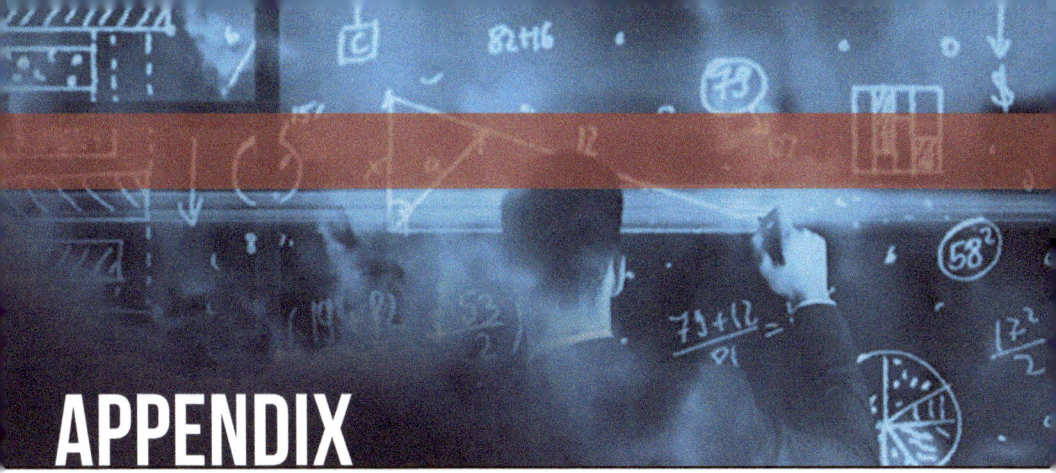

APPENDIX

Evolution of IT Risk Management

IT risk management warrants consideration in every organization because IT is pervasive in every industry and everything we do. The evolution of modern IT risk management began with the Project Management Institute (PMI) publishing the first edition of the *Project Management Body of Knowledge* (PMBOK) in 1987. While the PMBOK has changed significantly since 1987, the risk management elements have remained relatively unchanged. As an active member of PMI and frequent volunteer for PMI workshops, I continually strive to improve PMI's approach to risk management. PMI created the Risk Management Professional (RMP) certification, which is a step in the right direction. PMI's RMP and PMBOK are still focused on the tactical elements of risk management and do not include adequate treatment of the strategic governance elements of risk management. Unfortunately, PMI still lags behind the international risk management standards community.

Other international organizations such as ISO and ISACA have significantly expanded risk management practices into governance and improvement. *Figure 25* shows the evolution of IT risk management over the past couple decades and maps three risk management standards against the first edition of the PMBOK: Australia-New Zealand AS/NZS-4360, ISO/IEC 16085 Systems and software engineering – Lifecycle processes – Risk Management, and ISACA's Risk IT. As you can see in the diagram, there have been a number of improvements in risk management standards and industry best practices since 2004 mainly in the area of governance.

You will notice that all four organizations have the same core activities for governance, risk analysis, and risk treatment. Some organizations decompose activities whereas others combine similar activities. For example, the PMBOK and Risk IT include all risk response planning in a single activity. AN/NZS 4360 and ISO 16085, on the other hand, break down risk response planning activities into two separate activities. There are subtle differences between these four organizations but fundamentally they offer consistent guidance across the board. However, you will notice that risk management begins to evolve in 2004 when AN/NZS 4360 began to decompose risk management activities and provide more granular detail. AN/NZS 4360 aligned very closely with the PMBOK risk analysis processes but expanded the governance and risk treatment aspects of risk management. ISO 16085 followed two years later and borrowed heavily from AS/NZS 4360. ISO 16085 expands on governance activities even further and introduced the improvement category, which is dedicated to risk management process improvement.

A number of significant changes to risk management came along in 2009 with the release of ISACA's Risk IT framework and practice guide. Risk IT was a revolutionary change to IT risk management. Risk IT significantly expanded the governance aspects of risk management, suggested that improvement activities begin in the governance and definition phase, introduced the concept of risk scenarios, and presented a simplified risk prioritization scheme that I have become a big fan of. Read my book *Chaos to Clarity: The Tao of Risk Management* to learn more about the tactical, practical elements of risk management.

	1987 PMBOK	2004 AN/NZS 4360	2006 ISO 16085	2009 RISK IT
GOVERNANCE	• Risk Management Planning	• Establish Context • Communicate & Consult	• Manage the Project Risk Profile • Plan & Implement Risk Management	• Risk Awareness, Communication & Reporting • Define Risk Universe & Scope Risk Management • Risk Appetite & Tolerance
RISK ANALYSIS	• Risk Identification • Qualitative Analysis • Quantitative Analysis	• Identify Risks • Analyze Risks • Evaluate Risks	• Risk Analysis	• Expressing & Describing Risk • Risk Scenarios
RISK TREATMENT	• Risk Response Planning	• Treat Risks • Monitor & Review Risk Events	• Treat Risks • Monitor & Review Risk Events	• Risk Response & Prioritization
IMPROVEMENT			• Evaluate Risk Management Process	• Risk Awareness, Communication & Reporting

Figure 26: Evolution of Risk Management

Annotated Glossary

This glossary provides a list of common risk terms. Many terms include an extended description along with one or more examples to help illustrate the term and associated concepts.

Accept: Risk management strategy where a conscious decision is made to accept the risk. Accepted risk events are also a subset of the known-known risk events. Acceptance is commonly used where the impact of the risk event is projected to be less than the cost to treat and manage the risk. Factoring the impact of accepted risks into the contingency reserve is the most effective way to manage the overall impact to the organization. Accepted risk events must be documented in the risk register and continually reviewed to confirm that the probability and impact has not changed. Risk events are rarely static, so probability of occurrence and impact are likely to change over time. Accepted risk events often go undocumented because they are perceived as fully treated. However, organizational appetite and tolerance can change over time, or an accepted risk event can evolve to the point that the impact exceeds the threshold of acceptable risk. Therefore, it is imperative that accepted risk events are documented and monitored in case a new treatment strategy is warranted.

Appetite: The amount of risk an organization can tolerate and justify in their pursuit of organizational goals and objectives. Risk appetite is defined in the Enterprise Risk Policy and should be quantitatively defined to avoid misinterpreting the organization's risk appetite. The risk policy should define organizational context elements and the specific appetite for each context.

Avoid: Risk management strategy that seeks to circumvent risk events entirely. For example, someone who seeks to avoid hurricane damage to a new house would build the house outside of the known hurricane zone(s), possibly in a non-coastal state. To avoid a project risk event, an organization could simply cancel or de-scope the requirement(s) associated with the risk event. There are clearly substantial costs associated with risk avoidance, not to mention potential lost opportunities. Risk avoidance is typically found in highly conservative, risk-averse organizations. Risk avoidance can be quite costly, so it is important to take this factor into account when planning for risk management. Many organizations are sensitive to the fact that they are risk averse, and the organizational culture tends to shy away from formally documenting risk events or threat events that they choose to avoid. To effectively manage risk in a risk averse organization, it is important to confirm that the risk policy accurately reflects the risk sensitivity of both the organization and key stakeholders so that realistic treatment plans can be developed.

Known-known: A "known" is an item or situation containing no uncertainty (Wideman, 1992). Therefore, a known-known is a situation or circumstance that is fully expected to occur; however, the actual timing and frequency of occurrence may not be fully known. One can make a case that a known-known should be handled as an issue. Whether to classify a known-known as a risk event or an issue is less important than documenting and managing it through a defined process.

Known-unknown: Risk events that can be reasonably expected to impact a given project, although the degree of impact and probability of occurrence cannot be immediately determined. The total impact of the known-unknowns should be used to ascertain the size of the contingency reserve. The contingency reserve should be expressed in terms of all assets that can be applied, not just budgets.

Mitigate: Risk treatment strategy where a risk treatment plan is prepared. A risk treatment plan is based on a mitigation strategy or series of actions that can reduce the impact of the risk to some degree. A frequent problem with risk policies or risk management plans is that they are often based on the false assumption that all risk events must be mitigated. It is unreasonable to expect that all risk events can be mitigated, and it may not be feasible or cost effective to mitigate a given risk event. The key to effective risk management is to recognize that risk events must be managed and treated even though they cannot be fully mitigated. Risk control is a term that is frequently used synonymously with mitigation. Risk control is a terminology problem that should be avoided. It is nearly impossible to control a risk event; the best that one can hope for is to recognize the impact of a risk event and take steps to minimize the impact.

Primary risk: A specific risk event that can be documented and quantified. Primary risk is usually the only type of risk that is identified on a consistent basis; very few organizations are mature enough to effectively manage residual and secondary risk.

Residual risk: Risk that remains after risk treatment actions have been completed (Project Management Institute, 2008, p.438). Residual risk is another case where industry organizations use the same term to mean slightly different things. Some organizations define residual risk as risk that remains after implementing internal controls. Residual risk can remain even after implementing internal controls and implementing risk treatment. Risk practitioners must be sensitive to the context that residual risk is used in so as not to confuse residual risk that exists after implementing internal controls and residual risk that exists after implementing risk treatment actions. In *Cultural Calamity*, residual risk is used to denote risk that exists after internal controls and risk treatment actions. Residual risk is risk that remains after treating a primary or secondary risk. Income protection is a good example of residual risk. To illustrate residual risk let's assume that your monthly income is $10,000. Losing one's income from an accident or illness can be devastating to personal or family objectives. To reduce the effect of income loss, one may choose to transfer income loss risk by purchasing long-term disability (LTD) insurance. Many employers offer LTD that typically replaces two-thirds of your income. In this example, LTD provides $6,666.67 in disability income leaving $3,333.33 in residual risk. There is an important lesson here for organizations that transfer their risk. Transferring risk can be an effective strategy to reduce risk, but transferring risk does not eliminate all the risk.

Risk exposure: The total risk impact to an organization, typically represented by six categories: safety, reputation, schedule, budget, quality, or mission. Each risk event can represent some amount of safety, reputation, schedule, budget, quality, or mission risk. The sum total of all individual risk exposure represents the total organizational risk exposure that must be considered when making risk strategy decisions. Risk exposure is an essential element used to establish an organization's risk appetite and risk tolerance. The organization's risk policy should establish risk exposure thresholds the organization can tolerate and effectively manage.

Risk IT: Risk IT is a risk management framework from ISACA. Risk IT is focused on IT risk but applies to many areas other than IT. Much work is being done in Great Britain with risk scenarios very similar to those described in Risk IT. For example, the Warwickshire community defined nine risk scenarios, including industrial accidents, transport accidents, industrial technical failure, etc. Each risk scenario includes a number of risk events that could occur as part of the scenario, the impact on the community, the likelihood of occurrence, etc.

Risk management strategy: One of four industry strategies for managing risk treatment (accept, avoid, transfer, and mitigate). It is critical that the risk management process drives risk owners to make a conscious decision to select a specific risk management strategy. Many organizations default to mitigate as the primary strategy, and risk that is transferred, avoided, or accepted is entirely ignored. Risk events that are accepted transferred or avoided frequently result in secondary or residual risk. Therefore, regardless of the risk management strategy, it is imperative that all risk events are added to the risk register and actively managed irrespective of the treatment strategy. The risk treatment strategy is selected while prioritizing risk items or risk scenarios and is heavily influenced by the risk policy.

Risk Owner: A specific individual who is accountable for determining whether risk treatment is complete. The risk owner is also the individual who experiences the effects of a loss event and writes the check to cover the effects of the loss. The risk owner is often confused with the person(s) who are responsible for executing risk treatment actions. Therefore, it is essential to distinguish between action item owners and risk owners. Risk owners, in most cases, should be members of the C-suite (or equivalent) or board members because they are the individuals with authority to expend resources to cover losses. Risk owners must be able to commit strategic resources to treat risk events. Many organizations drive risk ownership to individuals deep within the organization. Driving risk ownership deep within an organization forces risk treatment to occur on a very tactical level without the benefit of having access to strategic resources. Tactically oriented risk management without the benefit of strategic assets often results in frequent loss events because owners do not have the authority to commit strategic resources. Risk owners who lack the authority to expend strategic assets are able to abdicate their responsibility in the matter and can shrug the matter off as a management problem.

Risk posture: The overarching approach for managing risk. It is comprised of technical policies, non-technical policies, governance, procedures, and controls that are intended to protect the organization from both internal and external threats.

Secondary risk: Risk that arises as a direct result of implementing a risk response (Project Management Institute, 2008, p. 441). Secondary risk is risk that is created by treating a risk event. The Deepwater Horizon disaster provides an excellent example of a secondary risk. The primary risk faced by British Petroleum (BP) was damage to shorelines, beaches, and wildlife. BP's risk response to this primary risk was to apply chemical compounds called "dispersants" to the oil floating on the surface of the water (Lustgarten, 2010). These dispersants cause oil on the surface to break up and sink to the bottom. However, the dispersants contain highly toxic chemicals that can kill fish and damage aquatic ecosystems. In implementing their risk response to the primary risk of shoreline damage, BP created a secondary risk of damage to the marine ecosystem.

Another example of secondary risk is the case where aluminum wiring was used to reduce budget risk during the building boom of the 1960s. The price of copper doubled between the years 1950 – 1956 and nearly doubled again between 1959 – 1970 sending homebuilders looking for a cheaper alternative (U.S. Geological Survey, 1999). The cheaper alternative turned out to be aluminum. Aluminum had similar characteristics to copper and was about the same price in 1959 but almost half the price of copper in 1970. Many homebuilders began to use aluminum wiring as a way to manage budget risk. However, what was unknown at the time was that this treatment action unknowingly introduced a significant safety risk.

Aluminum is a very soft metal that easily expands and contracts. Anyone who has used a toaster or other appliance knows that electricity running through wires can cause the wire to heat up; this is also true with aluminum wiring. Aluminum wiring expands as it heats up from electricity running through it and contracts as it cools. The constant expansion and contraction often causes a gap to form between the wire and the connector. The connection becomes hotter and hotter each time an electrical load is applied, until one day the connection gets hot enough to ignite surrounding material (Aluminum Wire Repair, Inc., 2016)

Tolerance: The amount of variance from the appetite threshold an organization is willing to tolerate. There is a close relationship between risk exposure, risk tolerance, and reserves. Reserve budgets are the total amount of reserve resources (e.g. budget, time, assets) an organization is prepared to reserve specifically for managing risk. Reserve budgets are heavily influenced by the organization's tolerance. An organization with a high-risk tolerance needs to allocate additional reserves to compensate for their high tolerance. Conversely, an organization with a low-risk tolerance can be much more conservative with their reserve budgets. Risk exposure is the amount of resources expended for risk treatment plus any residual risk.

Transfer: Risk treatment strategy where risk is transferred to a third party. Two common ways to transfer risk are subcontracting and buying insurance. Risk practitioners should not be fooled into thinking that risk transferred to a third party is sufficiently treated. The four steps to effectively treat transferred risks are: 1) decide to transfer a risk event or threat event, 2) document the risk event in the risk register, 3) identify secondary risk and 4) identify residual risk. Simply transferring risk doesn't mean it has been effectively treated; transferring a risk event may reduce the risk impact, but it must still be monitored and managed. Buying auto or homeowners insurance is a very simple example of risk transfer where residual risk is left over from the transfer in the form of a deductible. Subcontracting the development of a critical software module to a third party is another example where risk is transferred. Outsourcing the critical software module does not guarantee that the software module will function as required or even be delivered on time. Subcontracting typically does reduce risk to some degree but does not fully eliminate the risk.

True North: Term used to describe organizational culture that drives proper risk behavior, supports a risk management organization that makes extensive use of proven best practices. True North indicates the presence of a risk-aware culture that actively promotes the identification, reporting, and management of risk.

Unknown-unknown: Circumstances or outcomes that were not conceived of by an observer at a given point in time (Answers.com, n.d.). An unknown-unknown is also referred to as a Black Swan event. Black Swan theory is based on Nassim Nicholas Taleb's article *The Black Swan: The Impact of the Highly Improbable* describing extreme events that cannot be reasonably conceived to happen (Taleb, 2007). Black Swan events are very rare occurrences that have far-reaching impact. The plague that ravaged Medieval Europe, 9/11 and the 2004 Indonesian Tsunami are examples of Black Swan events. These types of events are nearly impossible to plan for because the probability, frequency, and impact simply cannot be estimated. Management reserves are used to cope with Black Swan events. Highly mature organizations use modeling and simulation, gaming, and desktop exercises to help determine the amount of management reserve they should maintain.

Recommended Reading

There are a number of excellent risk management books and papers that provide insight into effective risk management. Following are books, papers, and articles I find most useful and interesting:

Chaos to Clarity: The Tao of Risk Management

Davis, M. (2012). Lessons Unlearned: The Legal and Policy Legacy of the BP Deepwater Horizon Spill. *Washington and Lee Journal of Energy, Climate, and the Environment, 3*(2), 155-170.

Douglas W. Hubbard entitled *The Failure of Risk Management, Why it's Broken and How to Fix It.*

Sutcliffe, K. M. (2011, June). High reliability organizations (HROs). *Best Practice & Research Clinical Anaesthesiology, 25*(2), 133-144.

Taleb, N. (2007, April 22). The Black Swan: The Impact of the Highly Improbable. *The New York Times.* Retrieved from

HM Treasury. (2004). *The Orange Book Management of Risk - Principles and Concepts.* Norwich, UK: HM Treasury.

Bibliography

Aluminum Wire Repair, Inc. (2016). Aluminum Wiring: What's the Problem. Retrieved from http://www.alwirerepair.com/aluminum-wiring-whats-the-problem

Answers.com. (n.d.). *Unknown Unknowns*. Retrieved from http://www.answers.com/topic/unknown-unknown

Basu, T. (2014, March). Timeline: A History Of GM's Ignition Switch Defect. *National Public Radio*, ().

Bea, R. G. (2011, January). Risk Assessment and Management: Challenges of the Macondo Well Blowout Disaster. *Deepwater Horizon Study Group*, (5-35).

Bea, R. (2006). *APPROACHES TO ACHIEVE ADEQUATE QUALITY AND RELIABILITY*. Berkely, CA: Center for Catastrophic Risk Management.

Boehm, B., & Basili, V. (2001, January). Software Defect Reduction Top 10 List. *Software Management*, (), 135-137.

CBS News. (2010). Toyota "Unintended Acceleration" Has Killed 89. Retrieved from http://www.cbsnews.com/news/toyota-unintended-acceleration-has-killed-89/

Carr, L. J. (1932, September). Disaster and the Sequence-Pattern Concept of Social Change. *American Journal of Sociology*, *38*(2), 207-218.

Consumer Reports. (2016). *Takata Airbag Recall - Everything You Need To Know*. Retrieved from http://www.consumerreports.org/cro/news/2016/05/everything-you-need-to-know-about-the-takata-air-bag-recall/index.htm#

Curwen, L. (2003, June 21). The corporate conscience: Sherron Watkins, Enron whistleblower. *The Guardian*, p. 1.

Davis, M. (2012). Lessons Unlearned: The Legal and Policy Legacy of the BP Deepwater Horizon Spill. *Washington and Lee Journal of Energy, Climate, and the Environment*, *3*(2), 155-170.

DeCarlo, S., & VanderMey, A. (2015, May). The 14 longest serving CEOs of the Fortune 500. *Fortune Magazine*, ().

Deepwater Horizon Study Group. (2011). *Final Report on the Investigation of the Macondo Well Blowout*. Berkley, CA: Deepwater Horizon Study Group.

Eilperin, J. (2010). "U.S. exempted BP's Gulf of Mexico drilling from environmental impact study". The Washington Post (The Washington Post Company).

Elsbach, K. D., Stigliani, I., & Stroud, A. (2011). *THE BUILDING OF EMPLOYEE DISTRUST: A CASE STUDY OF HEWLETT-PACKARD FROM 1995-2010*. Davis, CA: Graduate School of Management, University of California, Davis.

Enron "created fake trading room". (2002, February). *BBC News,* (), . Retrieved from http://goo.gl/Sjrg4q

Etkin, D. S. (1999). ESTIMATING CLEANUP COSTS FOR OIL SPILLS. *1999 International Oil Spill Conference*, (168).

European Commission. (1996). *Directive 96/82/EC "SEVESO II" Article 9(6)*. Brussels, Belgium: European Commission.

Finch, J. (2010). Toyota Sudden Acceleration: A Case Study of the National Highway Traffic Safety Administration - Recalls for Change. *Loyola Consumer Law Review*, *22*(4), 472-496.

Forliti, A. (2015, February 3). Jury: Toyota must pay $11M to victims of fatal crash. *The Seattle Times*, p. 2.

Halley, M.E. (1693). *An Estimate of the Degrees of the Mortality of Mankind, Drawn from Curious Tables of the Births and Funerals at the City of Breslaw; With an Attempt to Ascertain the Price of Annuities upon Lives*. Philosophical Transactions of the Royal Society of London, (), 596-610.

Healey, J. R. (2014, September 29). Feds look at new Toyota acceleration claims. *USA Today*, p. 1.

Hosaka, T. A. (2010, May 16). Toyota Recall: How Much Will It End Up Costing The Automaker?. *The Huffington Post*, p. 1.

House of Lords, . (2006, June). Government Policy on the Management of Risk. *Select Committee on Economic Affairs*, *1*(5th Report of Session 2005–06).

Hubbard, D. W. (2009). *The Failure of Risk Management: Why It's Broken and How to Fix It*. Hoboken, New Jersey: John Wiley & Sons, Inc.

Information Systems Audit and Control Association (ISACA). (2009). *The Risk IT Practitioner Guide*. Rolling Meadows, IL: Information Systems and Control Association (ISACA).

Information Systems Audit and Control Association (ISACA). (2015). *CRISC Review Manual* (6th ed.). Rolling Meadows, IL: Information Systems Audit and Control Association (ISACA).

Ingram, AD., Underwood, A., & Thompson, M. (2014, September). Risk Culture, Neoclassical Economics and Enterprise Risk Management. *2014 Enterprise Risk Management Symposium*, (), 1-12.

International Electrotechnical Commission. (2009). *International Standard IEC/ISO 31010, Risk management - Risk assessment techniques*. Geneva, Switzerland: International Electrotechnical Commission.

International Standards Organization. (2006). *International Standard ISO/IEC 16085, Systems and software engineering — Life cycle processes — Risk management*. Geneva, Switzerland: International Standards Organization.

Isidore, C. (2015, February). GM's Total Recall Cost: $4.1 billion. *CNN Money,* (),. Retrieved from http://money.cnn.com/2015/02/04/news/companies/gm-earnings-recall-costs/

Ishaq Bhatti, M., Awan, H. M., & Razaq, Z. (2014). The key performance indicators (KPIs) and their impact on overall organizational performance. *Quality and Quantity, 48*(6), 3127-3143. doi:http://dx.doi.org/10.1007/s11135-013-9945-y

Kaplan, R. S., & Mikes, A. (2012, June). Managing Risks: A New Framework. *Harvard Business Review*, ().

Kingsbury, K. (2008, May). The Value of a Human Life: $129,000. *Time*, (), 1.

KPMG. (2009). *Government IT Projects Need QA/IV&V.* : KPMG.

Krisher, T. (2016, July 13). Court Ruling Opens GM to Billions in Death, Injury Claims. *ABC News*, p. 1.

Kunreuther, H., Michel-Kerjan, E., & Useem, M.. (2013). *Corporate Strategies for Managing Catastrophic Risks in the S&P 500: Linking Intuitive and Deliberative Thinking.* Philadelphia, PA: Wharton School, University of Pennsylvania.

Leung, M. (n.d.). *Chronology of Probabilists and Statisticians.* University of Texas El Paso. Retrieved from http://www.math.utep.edu/Faculty/mleung/probabilityandstatistics/chronology.htm

Libuser, C. B. (1994). *Organizational structure and risk mitigation.* (Order No. 9427348, University of California, Los Angeles). *ProQuest Dissertations and Theses,* , 218-218 p. Retrieved from http://search.proquest.com/docview/304083303?accountid=458. (304083303).

Lofstedt, R. E., Ikeda, S., & Thompson, K. M. (2000). Risk Management across the Globe: Insights from a Comparative Look at Sweden, Japan, and the United States. *Risk Analysis*, *20*(2), 157 - 161.

Lohr, S. (1999, July 23). Setting Her Own Precedents; Hewlett's Chief Prefers the Path Less Traveled. *The New York Times*, p. 3.

Lustgarten, A. (2010, April). Chemicals Meant To Break Up BP Oil Spill Present New Environmental Concerns. *ProPUBLICA,* (), . Retrieved from http://www.propublica.org/article/bp-gulf-oil-spill-dispersants-0430

MacPherson, D. (2014, January). How Long Does It Take to Change a Culture?. *ModernSurvey* , ().

Marsh & McLennan Companies. (2014). *The New Reality of Risk: Measuring and Mitigating Reputational Risk.* New York, NY: Marsh LLC.

Martin, P. K. (2005). "Auditing the Risk Response Plan". Sponsoring a Project. Martin Training Associates. Books24x7. <http://common.books24x7.com/book/id_12615/book.asp> (accessed March 7, 2010)

Morgan, D., & Klayman, B. (2015, May 20). UPDATE 8-Takata doubling U.S. recall for defective air bags to 34 mln vehicles. *Reuters*, p. 1.

Nakashima, E. (2016, June 14). Russian government hackers penetrated DNC, stole opposition research on Trump. *The Washington Post*, p. 1.

National Aeronautics and Space Administration. (2003). *Columbia Accident Investigation Board*. Washington, D.C.: Government Printing Office.

Office of Management and Budget. (2016). *OMB Circular No. A-123, Management's Responsibility for Enterprise Risk Management and Internal Control*. Washington, D.C.: Office of Management and Budget.

Ponemon Institute. (2015). *2015 Cost of Data Breach Study: Global Analysis*. Traverse City, MI: Ponemon Institute LLC.

Project Management Institute, (2008). *A Guide to the Project Management Body of Knowledge* (4th ed.). Newtown Square, PA: Project Management Institute, Inc.

PwC. (2016). The Global Innovation 1000: Comparison of R&D Spending by Regions and Industries. Retrieved from http://www.strategyand.pwc.com/global/home/what-we-think/innovation1000/rd-intensity-vs-spend-2015

Risk. (n.d.). In *Merriam-Webster OnLine Search*. Retrieved from http://www.merriam-webster.com/dictionary/risk

Robertson, C., Schwartz, J., & PÉREZ-PEÑA, R. (2015, July 2). BP to Pay $18.7 Billion for Deepwater Horizon Oil Spill. The New York Times, p. 1.

Sachdev, A. (2003, May 20). Conference center last resort for Andersen. *Chicago Tribune*, p. 1.

Shahain, A. M., & Mahbod, A. (2007, November). Prioritization of key performance indicators. *International Journal of Productivity and Performance Management, 56*(3), 226-240.

Smith, N. C., & Quirk, M. (2004). From Grace to Disgrace: the Rise & Fall of Arthur Andersen. *Journal of Business Ethics Education, 1*(1).

Sokolnikoff, L.S., & Sokolnikoff, E.S. (1941). *Higher Mathematics for Engineers and Physicists* (2nd ed.). New York and London: McGraw-Hill Book Company, Inc.

Spector, M. (2015, December 10). GM Ignition-Switch Fund Offers $595 Million to Victims. *The Wall Street Journal*, p. 2.

Stapleton, T. (2012). *Data Breach Cost - Risks, costs and mitigation strategies for data breaches*. Schaumburg, IL: Zurich American Insurance Corporation.

Sullivan, J., & Beach, R. (2009, February). Improving project outcomes through operational reliability: A conceptual model. *International Journal of Project Management*, (27), 765-775.

Sutcliffe, K. M. (2011). High Reliability Organizations (HROs). *Best Practice & Research Clinical Anaesthesiology, 25*(2), 133-144.

Taleb, N. (2007, April 22). The Black Swan: The Impact of the Highly Improbable. *The New York Times*. Retrieved from http://www.nytimes.com/2007/04/22/books/chapters/0422-1st-tale.html?_r=1&ex=1178769600&en=bdae1078f2b4a98c&ei=5070

The Council Of The European Communities. (1989). *Official Journal of the European Communities - Council Directive 89/391/EEC*. Luxembourg, : THE COUNCIL OF THE EUROPEAN COMMUNITIES.

Trop, J. (2013, October 25). Toyota Agrees to Settlement in Fatal Acceleration Crash. *The New York Times*, p. 1.

Turner, B. A. (1976). The Organizational and Interorganizational Development of Disasters. *Administrative Science Quarterly, 21*(3), 378-397.

The Open Group. (2014). *Pocket Guide The Open FAIR Body of Knowledge*. Reading, Berkshire: The Open Group.

U.S. Geological Survey. (1999). *Metal Prices in the United States Through 1998*. Washington, D.C.: United States Government Printing Office.

Valant, J. (2015). *Consumer protection in the EU - Policy Overview*. Brussels, : European Union.

Vlasic, B., & Apuzzo, M. (2014, March 19). Toyota Is Fined $1.2 Billion for Concealing Safety Defects. *The New York Times*, p. 1.

Wideman, R. M. (1992). Project & Risk Management A Guide to Managing Project Risks & Opportunities. Newtown Square, PA: Project Management Institute, Inc.

Index

www.ingramcontent.com/pod-product-compliance
Lightning Source LLC
Chambersburg PA
CBHW042121190326
41519CB00031B/7567